PIANO · VOCAL · GUITAR

2ND EDITION

LOVE SONGS FROM THE MOVIES

T0053083

ISBN-13: 978-0-7935-3312-1
ISBN-10: 0-7935-3312-0

HAL•LEONARD®
CORPORATION

7777 W. BLUEMOUND RD. P.O. BOX 13819 MILWAUKEE, WI 53213

Visit Hal Leonard Online at
www.halleonard.com

CONTENTS

ALL FOR LOVE

from Walt Disney Pictures' THE THREE MUSKETEERS

Words and Music by BRYAN ADAMS,
R.J. LANGE and MICHAEL KAMEN

be there when ___ you're old, to have and ___ to
from the wind and ___ the rain, from the hurt and ___ to
When hon - or's ___ at stake, this vow I ___ will

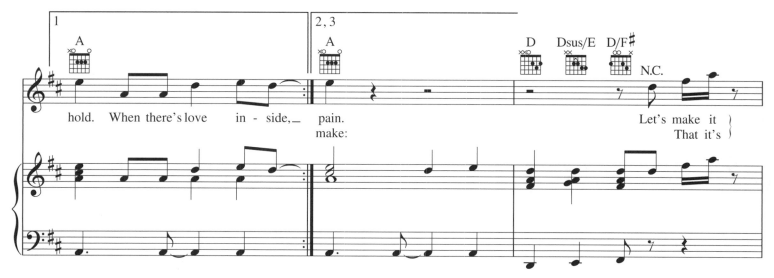

hold. When there's love in - side, ___ pain.
make:

Let's make it
That it's

all for one and all for love. _____

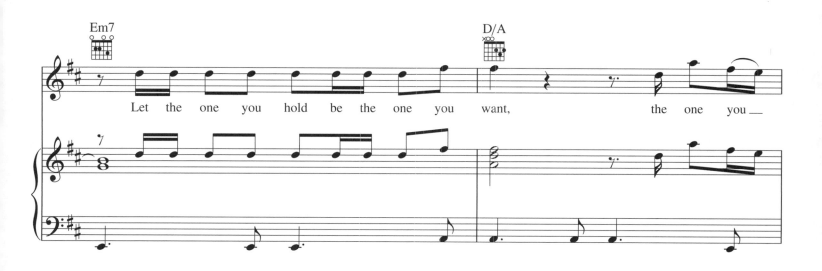

Let the one you hold be the one you want, the one you ___

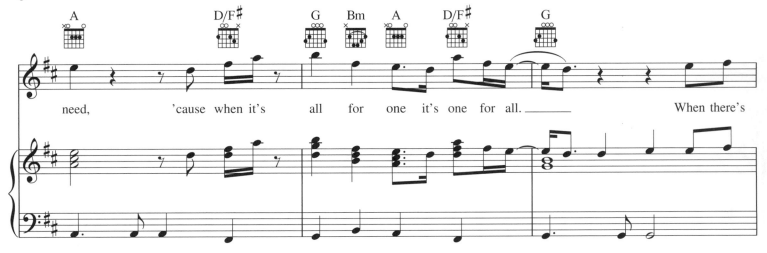

need, 'cause when it's all for one it's one for all. _____ When there's

some - one that should know, then just let your feel - ings show and make it

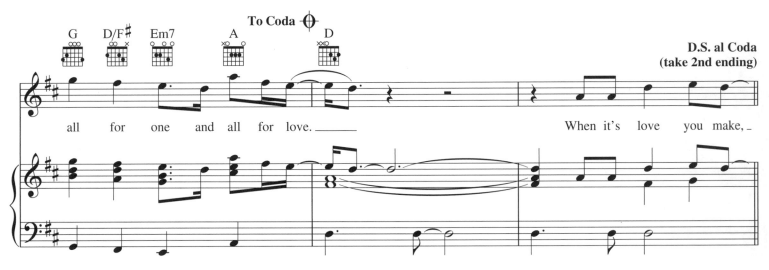

To Coda ⊕

D.S. al Coda
(take 2nd ending)

all for one and all for love. _____ When it's love you make, _

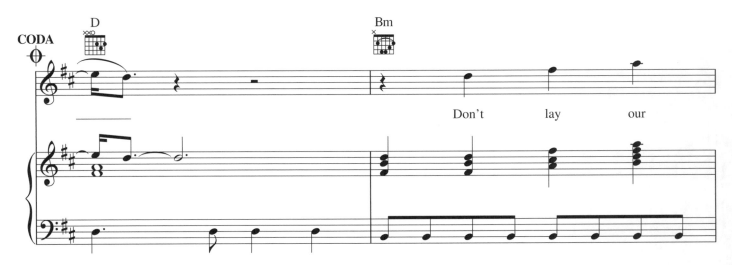

CODA ⊕

Don't lay our

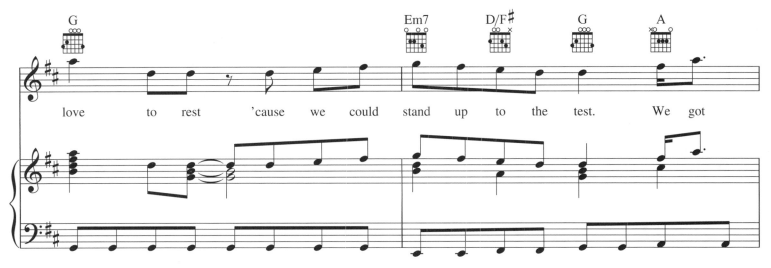

love to rest 'cause we could stand up to the test. We got

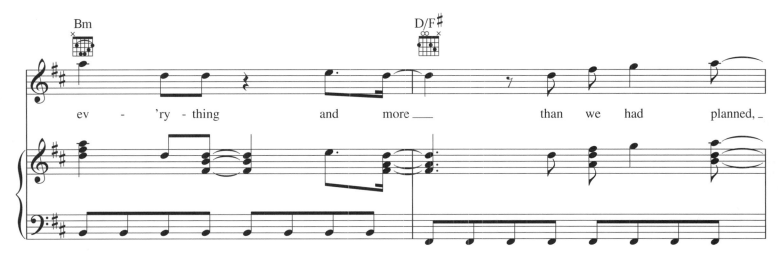

ev - 'ry - thing and more ___ than we had planned, ___

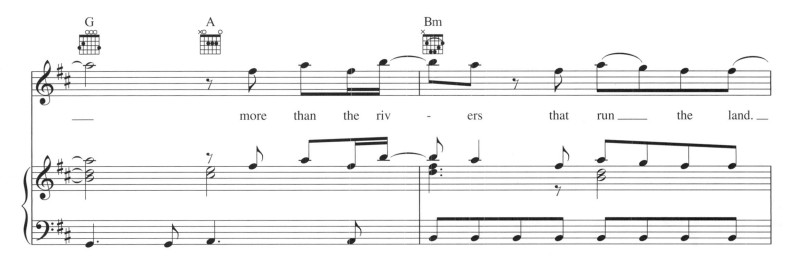

___ more than the riv - ers that run ___ the land. ___

___ We've got it all _____ in our hands.

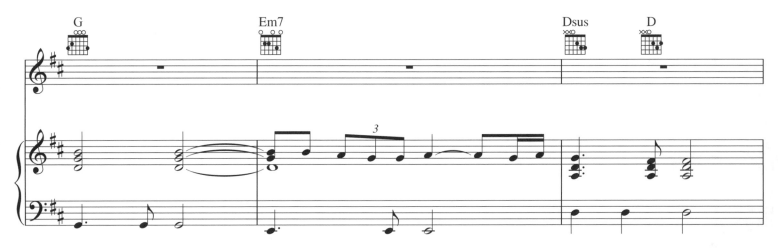

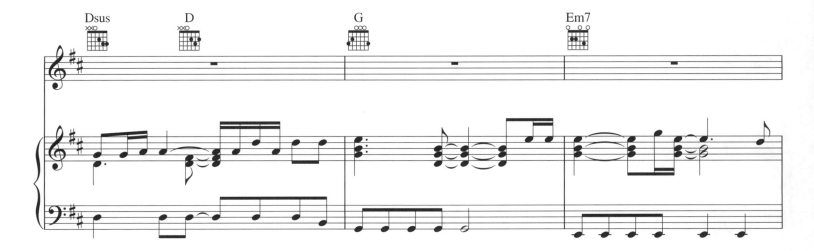

Now it's all for one and all for love. __

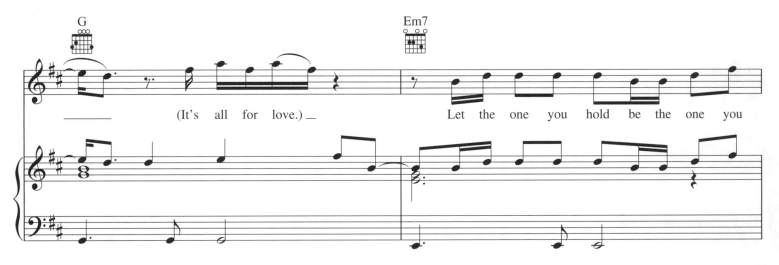

_____ (It's all for love.) __ Let the one you hold be the one you

ALL MY LOVING

from A HARD DAY'S NIGHT

Words and Music by JOHN LENNON
and PAUL McCARTNEY

Close your eyes and I'll kiss you, to-
tend that I'm kiss-ing the

mor-row I'll miss you; re-mem-ber I'll
lips I am miss-ing and hope that my

al-ways be true.
dreams will be come true. And then

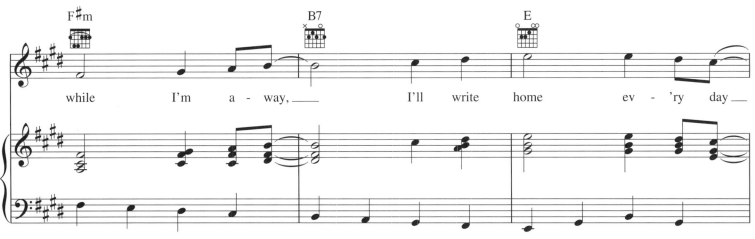

while I'm a-way,___ I'll write home ev-'ry day___

___ and I'll send all my lov-ing___ to

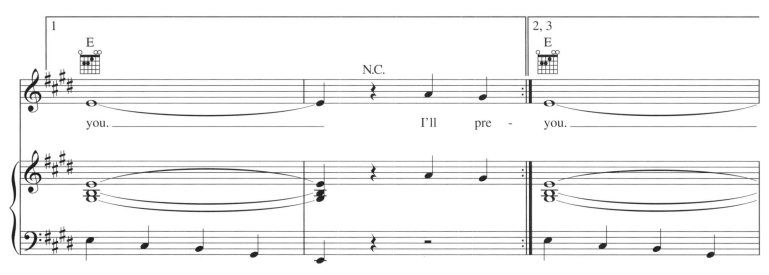

you.___ I'll pre - you.___

___ All my lov-ing___ I___ will send to

you, _____ all ___ my lov - ing, ___ dar-

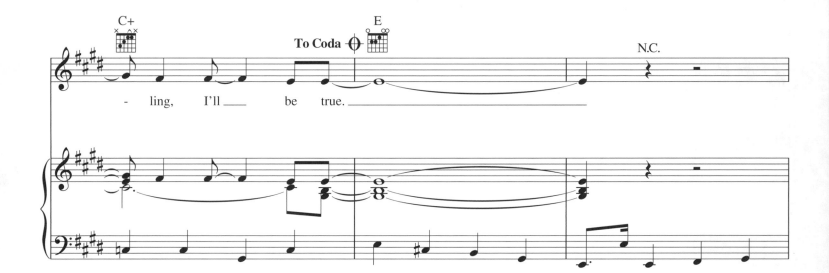

- ling, I'll ___ be true. _____

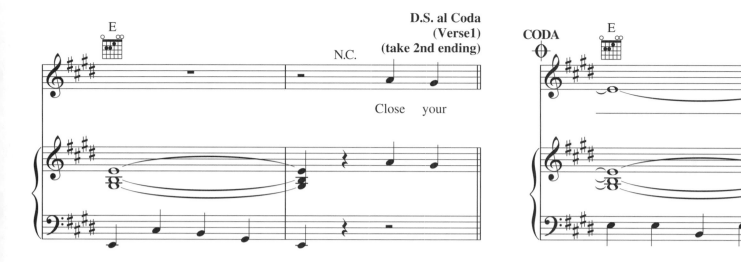

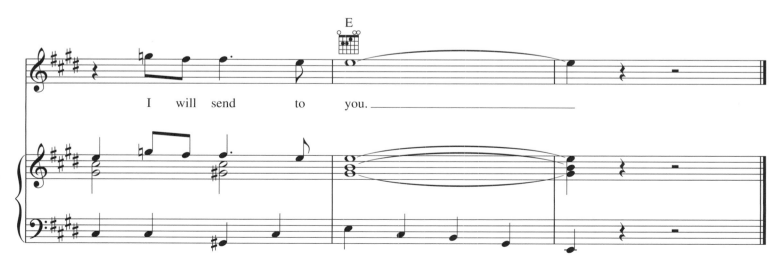

ALL THE WAY
from THE JOKER IS WILD

Words by SAMMY CAHN
Music by JAMES VAN HEUSEN

ALMOST PARADISE

Love Theme from the Paramount Motion Picture FOOTLOOSE

Words by DEAN PITCHFORD
Music by ERIC CARMEN

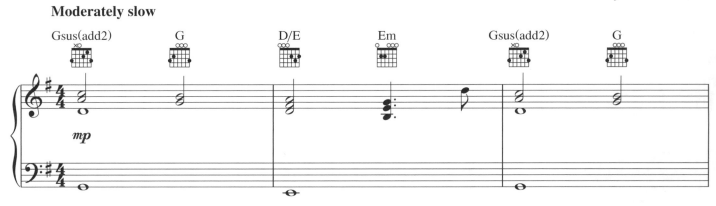

Moderately slow

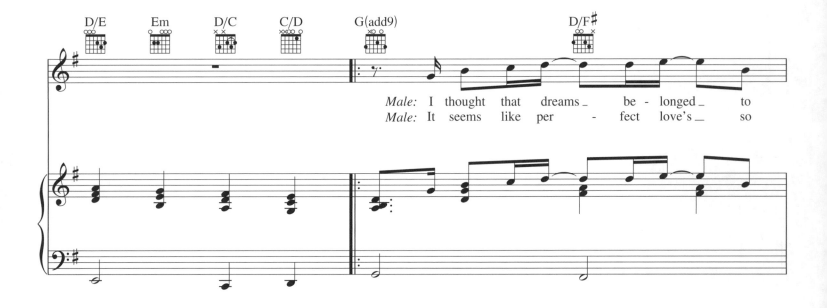

Male: I thought that dreams __ be - longed __ to
Male: It seems like per - fect love's __ so

oth - er men, ___ 'cause each time I ___ got close ___ they'd
hard to find. ___ I'd al - most giv - en up. ___ You

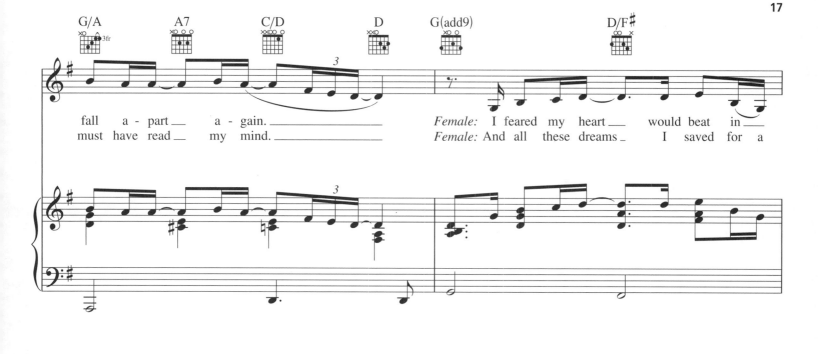

fall a - part __ a - gain. _____ *Female:* I feared my heart __ would beat in __
must have read __ my mind. _____ *Female:* And all these dreams _ I saved for a

se - cre - cy. __ I faced the nights ___ a - lone. _____ *Both:* Oh,
rain - y day, __ they're fi - n'lly com - ing true. _____ *Both:* I'll

how could I _____ have known that all my life __ I on - ly need - ed you?
share them all ___ with you, 'cause now we hold __ the fu - ture in __ our hands. _

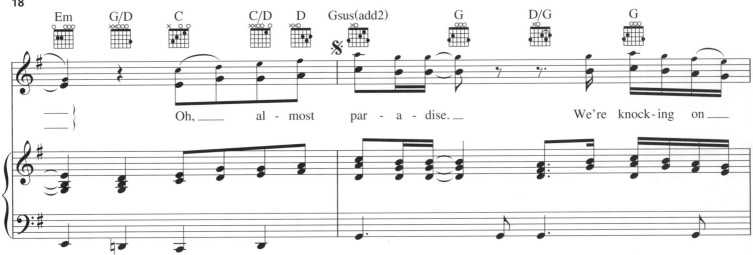

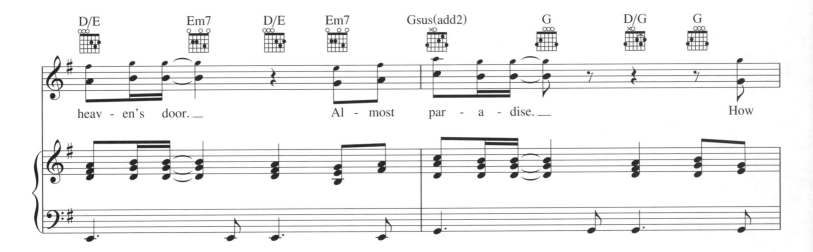

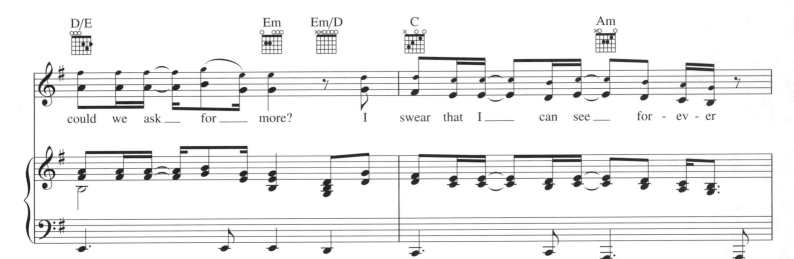

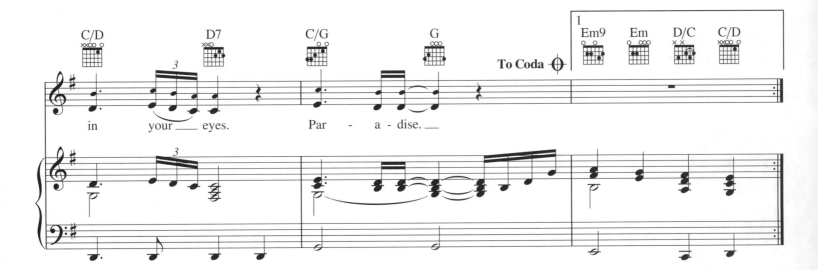

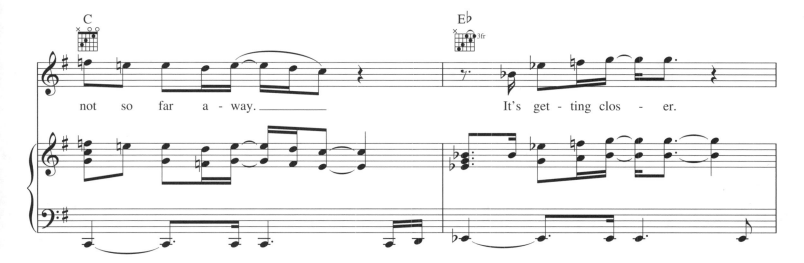

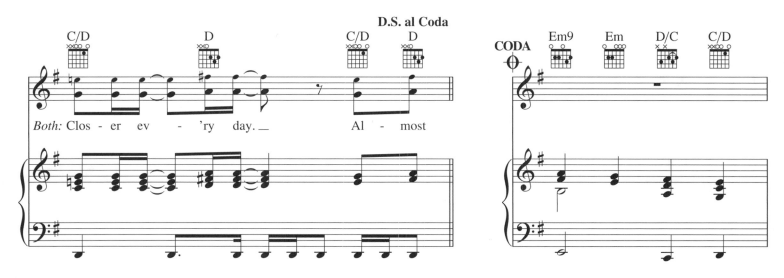

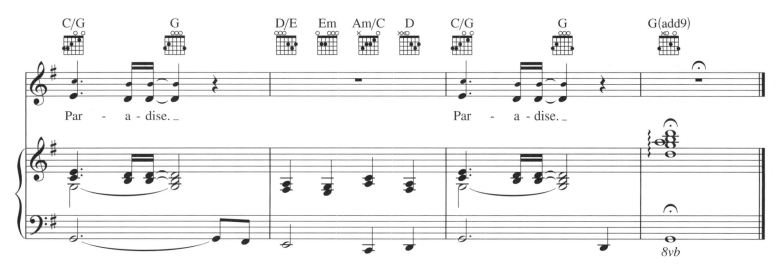

CAN YOU FEEL THE LOVE TONIGHT

from Walt Disney Pictures' THE LION KING

Music by ELTON JOHN
Lyrics by TIM RICE

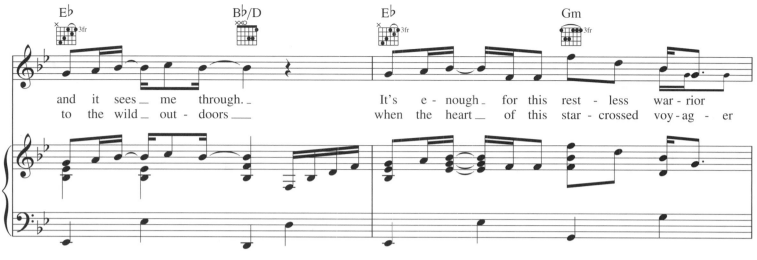

and it sees __ me through.   It's e-nough __ for this rest-less war-rior
to the wild __ out-doors __   when the heart __ of this star-crossed voy-ag-er

just to be __ with you. __   And can you feel __ the love __
beats in time __ with yours. __

poco cresc.

__ to-night? _____   It is where __ we are. __

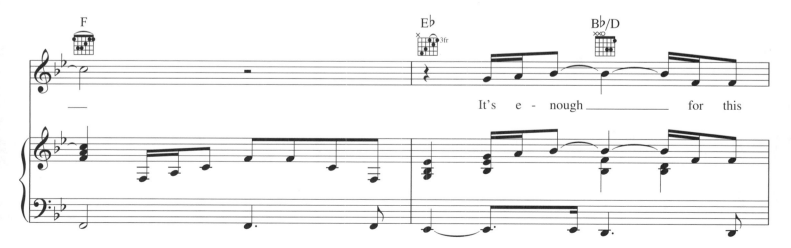

It's e-nough _____ for this

wide - eyed _____ wan - der - er that we got this far. _____

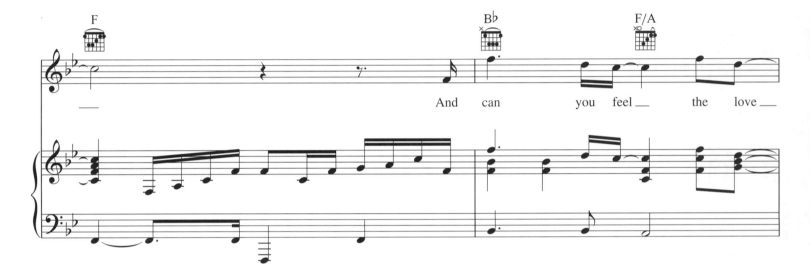

_____ And can you feel _____ the love _____

_____ to - night, _____ how it's laid _____ to rest? _____

_____ It's e - nough _____ to make

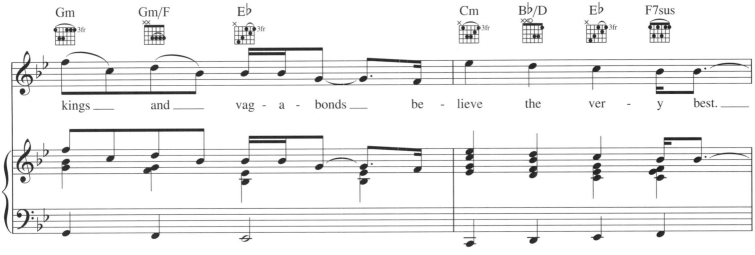

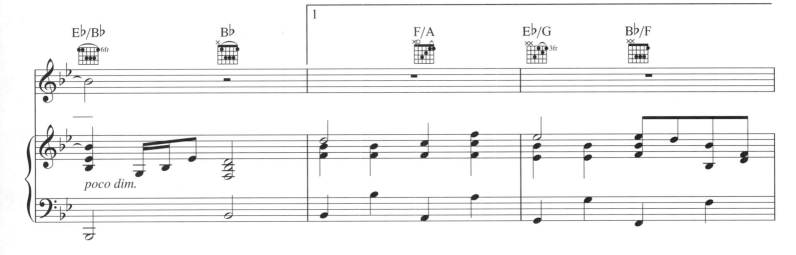

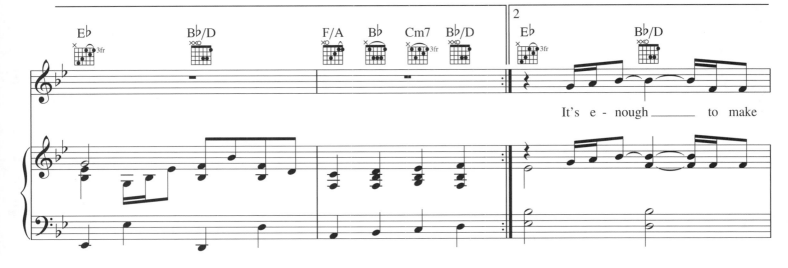

CAN'T HELP FALLING IN LOVE

from the Paramount Picture BLUE HAWAII

Words and Music by GEORGE DAVID WEISS,
HUGO PERETTI and LUIGI CREATORE

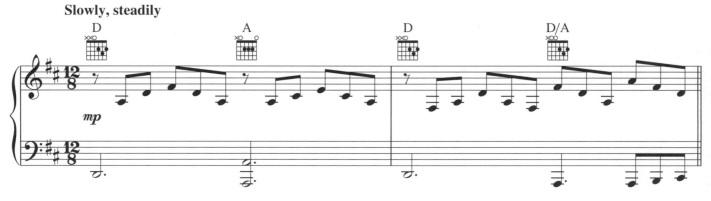

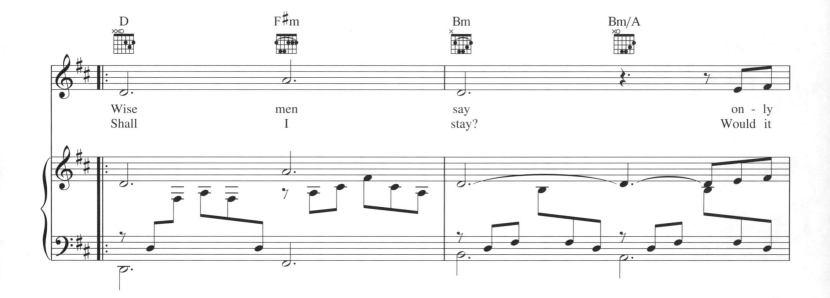

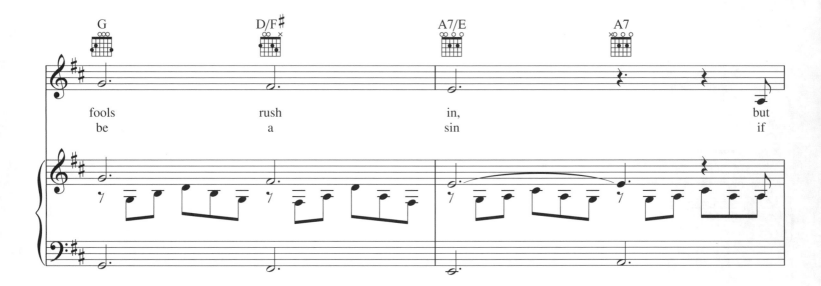

COULD I HAVE THIS DANCE
from URBAN COWBOY

Words and Music by WAYLAND HOLYFIELD
and BOB HOUSE

I'll al-ways re-mem-ber the song they were
al-ways re-mem-ber that mag-ic

play-ing the first time _____ we danced and I knew.
mo-ment, when I held _____ you close to me.

As we swayed to the mu-sic _____ and held to each
As we moved to-geth-er, _____ I knew for -

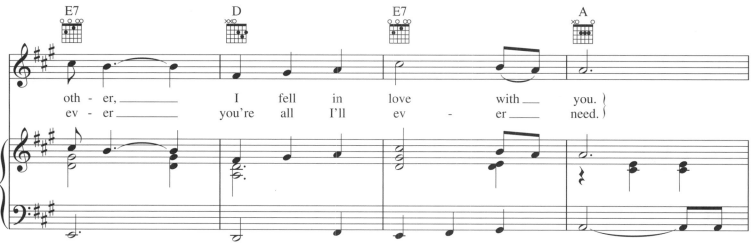

other, _____ I fell in love with ___ you.
ev - er _____ you're all I'll ev - er ___ need.

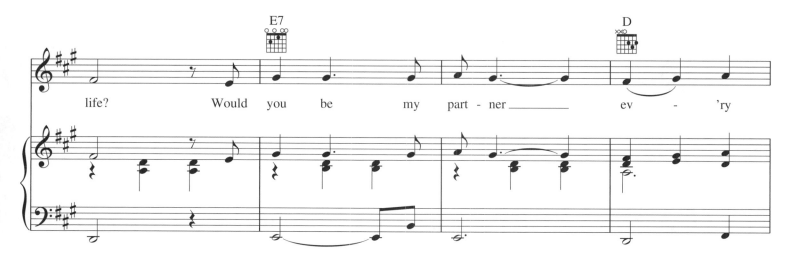

Could I have this dance for the rest of my

life? Would you be my part - ner _____ ev - 'ry

night? When we're to - geth - er, it feels ___ so

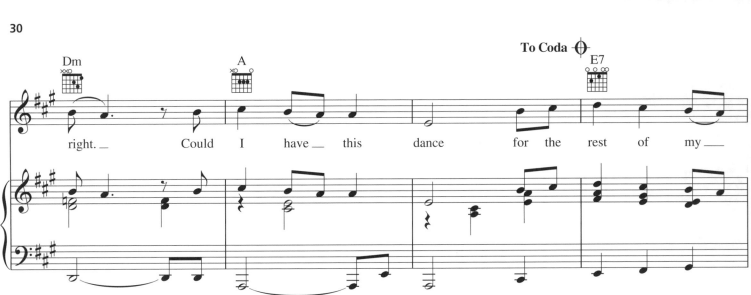

right. ___ Could I have ___ this dance for the rest of my ___

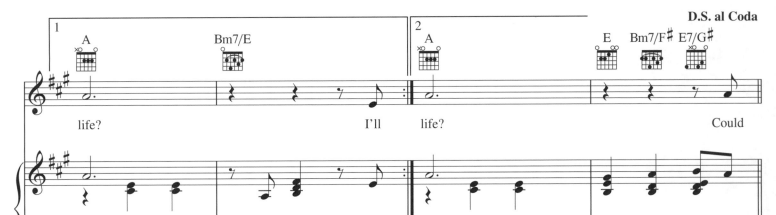

life? I'll life? Could

rest of my ___ life? ___

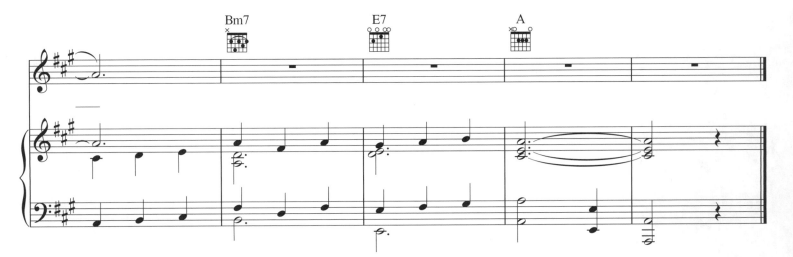

(Everything I Do)
I DO IT FOR YOU

from the Motion Picture ROBIN HOOD: PRINCE OF THIEVES

Words and Music by BRYAN ADAMS,
R.J. LANGE and MICHAEL KAMEN

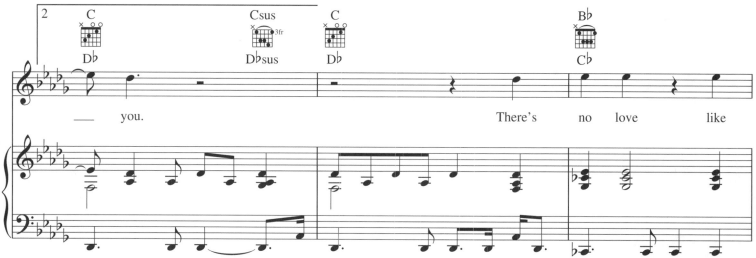

you. There's no love like

your love, _____ and no oth - er could give

more _____ love. There's no _____ way, _____ un - less

you're _____ there all the time, _____ all the

way, ___ yeah. _____

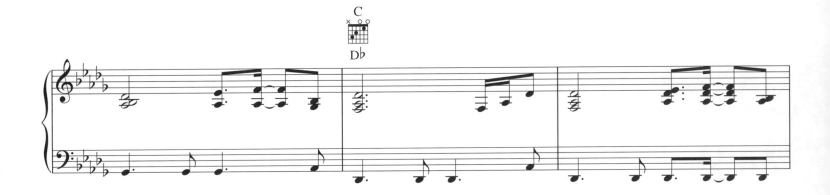

Oh, you can't tell me it's not worth try - ing for. I can't

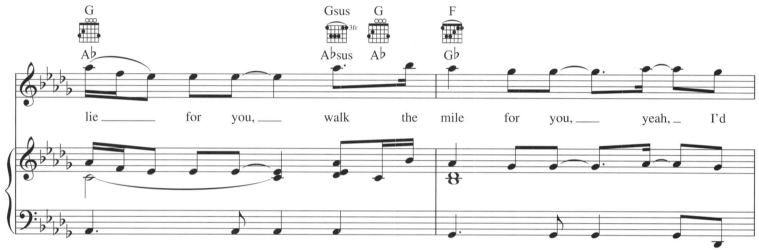

DO YOU KNOW WHERE YOU'RE GOING TO?

Theme from MAHOGANY

Words by GERRY GOFFIN
Music by MICHAEL MASSER

Moderately, with expression

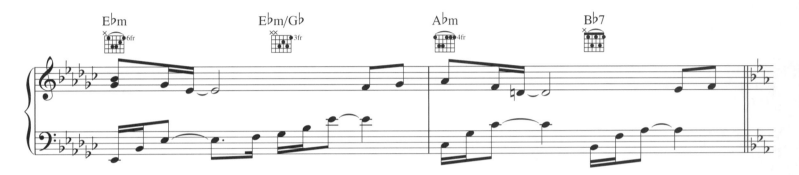

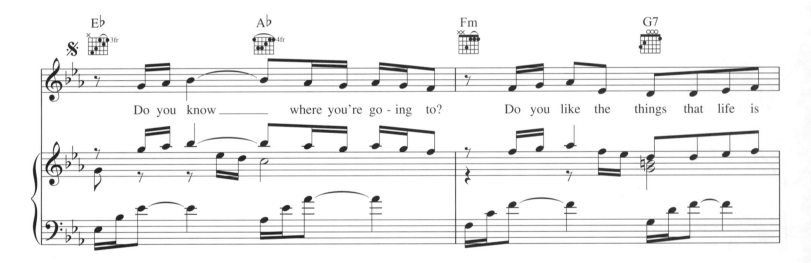

Do you know _____ where you're go-ing to? Do you like the things that life is

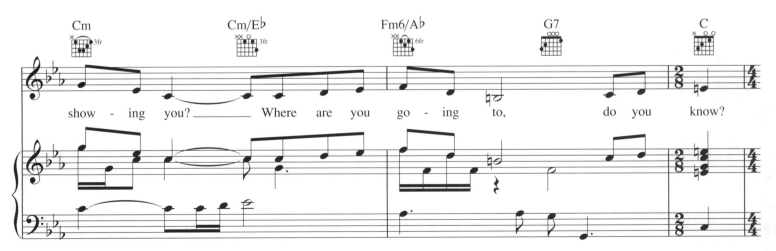

show - ing you? _____ Where are you go-ing to, do you know?

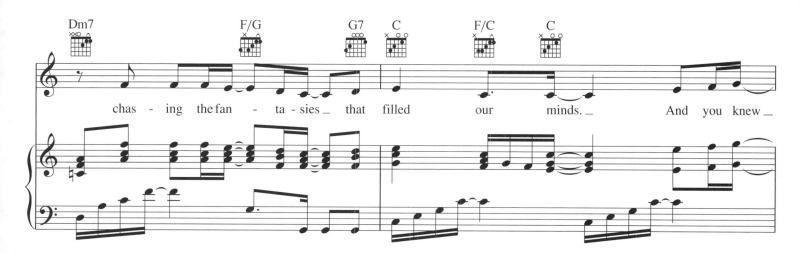

how I loved you but __ my spir - it was free,

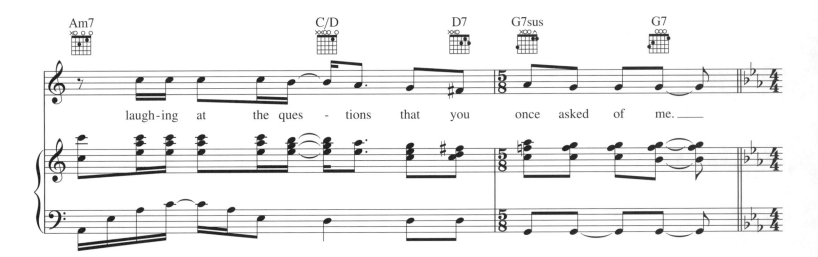

laugh-ing at the ques - tions that you once asked of me. __

Do you know __ where you're go - ing to? Do you like the things that life is

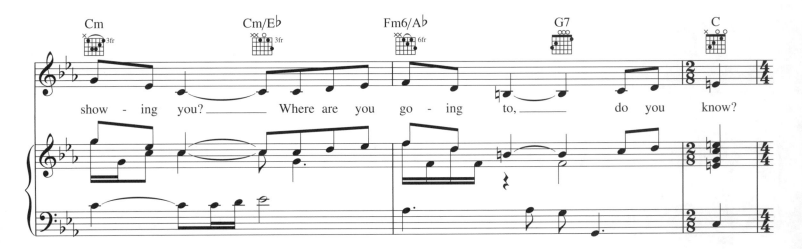

show - ing you? __ Where are you go - ing to, __ do you know?

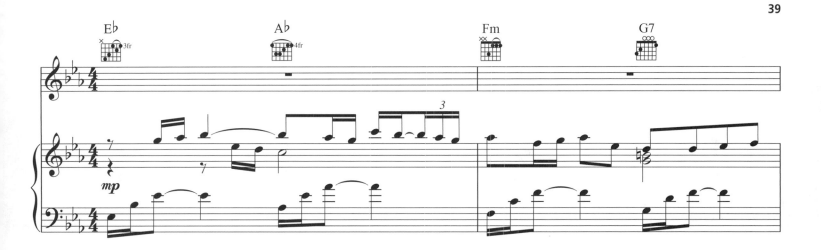

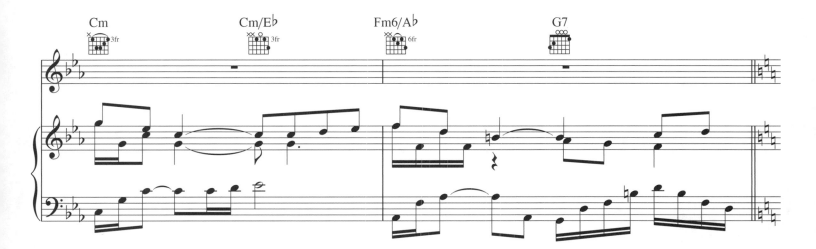

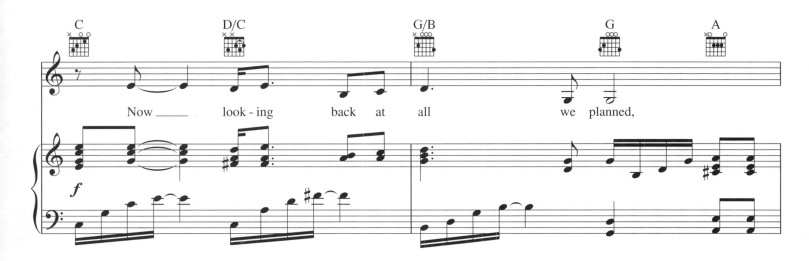

Now _____ look-ing back at all _____ we planned,

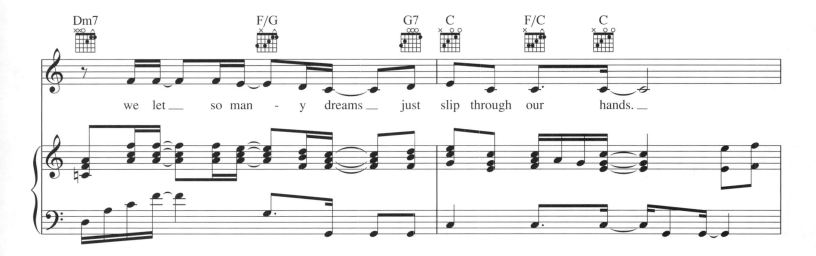

we let _____ so man - y dreams _____ just slip through our _____ hands. _____

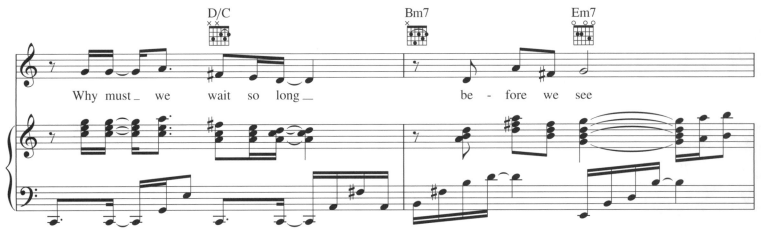

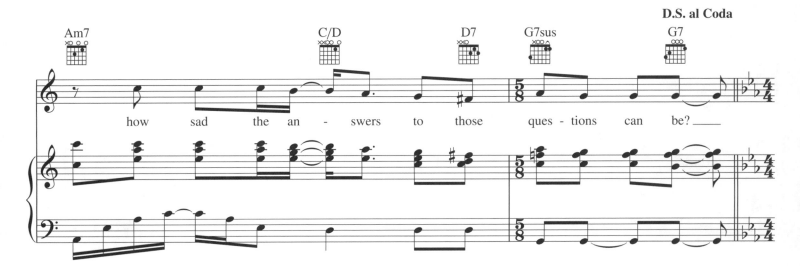

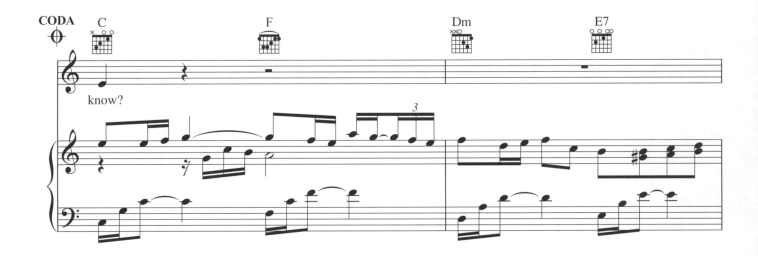

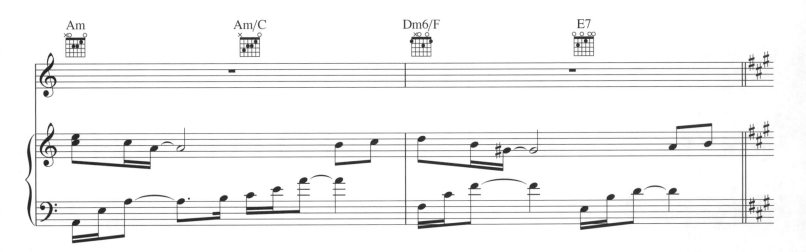

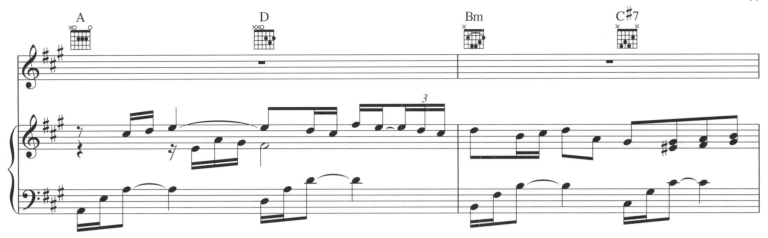

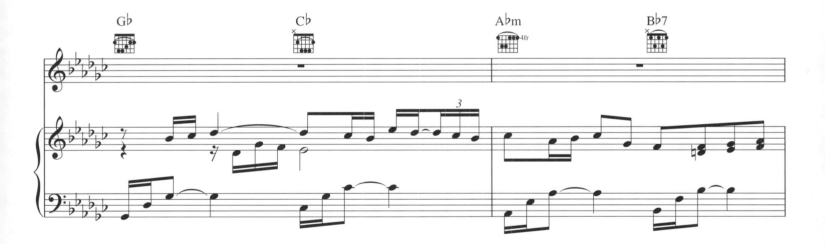

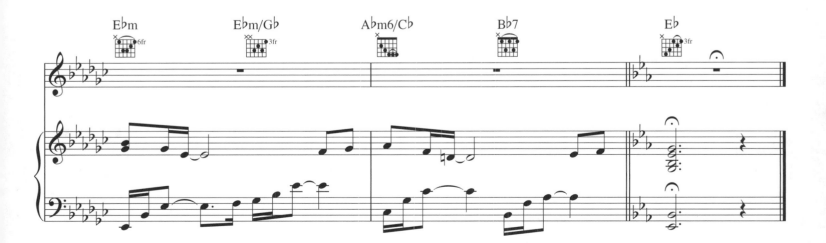

END OF THE ROAD

from the Paramount Motion Picture BOOMERANG

Words and Music by BABYFACE,
L.A. REID and DARYL SIMMONS

Why do you play with my heart? Why do you play with my mind? _____
You've nev - er been there be - fore, it's on - ly your first time. _____

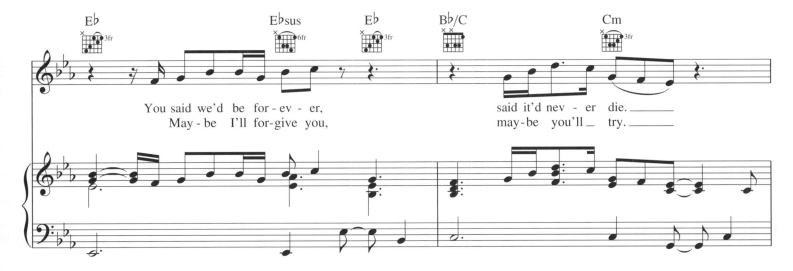

You said we'd be for - ev - er, said it'd nev - er die. _____
May - be I'll for - give you, may - be you'll _ try. _____

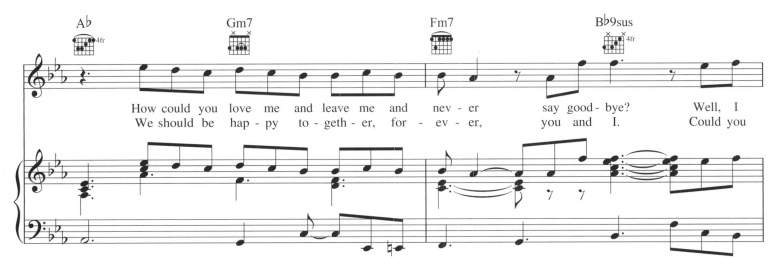

How could you love me and leave me and nev - er say good - bye? Well, I
We should be hap - py to - geth - er, for - ev - er, you and I. Could you

can't sleep at night with - out hold - ing you tight. Girl, each time I try I just break down and cry.
love me a - gain like you loved me be - fore? This time I want you to love me much more.

(1.) Pain in my head, oh, I'd rath-er be dead, spin-nin' a-round and a-round.
(2.,3.) This time in-stead, just come to my bed _____ and, ba-by, just don't let me down. _ } Al-though we've

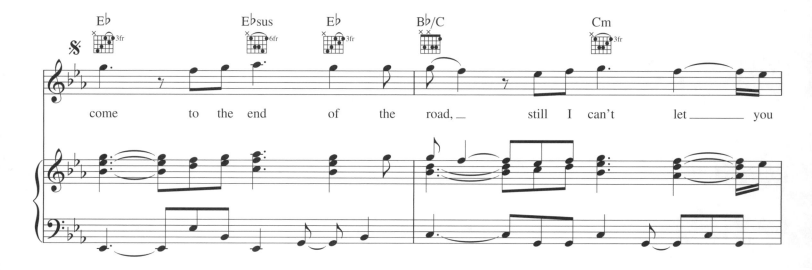

come to the end of the road, _ still I can't let _____ you

go. _ It's un-nat-u-ral. You be-long to me, I be-long to you. _

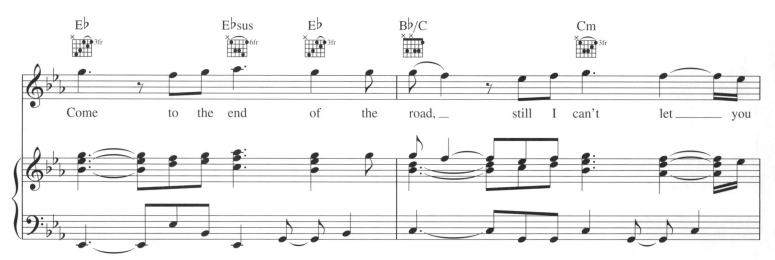

Come to the end of the road, _ still I can't let _____ you

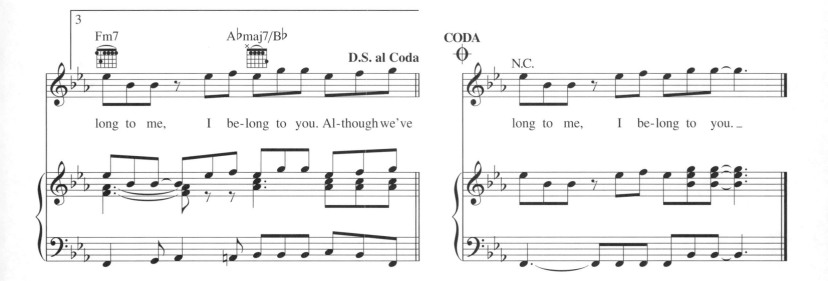

Additional Lyrics

(Spoken:) *Girl, I'm here for you.*
All those times at night when you just hurt me,
And just ran out with that other fellow,
Baby, I knew about it.
I just didn't care.
You just don't understand how much I love you, do you?
I'm here for you.
I'm not out to go out there and cheat all night just like you did, baby.
But that's alright, huh, I love you anyway.
And I'm still gonna be here for you 'til my dyin' day, baby.
Right now, I'm just in so much pain, baby.
'Cause you just won't come back to me, will you?
Just come back to me.

Yes, baby, my heart is lonely.
My heart hurts, baby, yes, I feel pain too.
Baby, please...

ENDLESS LOVE

from ENDLESS LOVE

Words and Music by
LIONEL RICHIE

Moderately slow

My love, __ there's on-ly you in my life, __
Two hearts, __ two hearts that beat as __ one; __

the on-ly thing that's right. __
our lives have just be-gun. __

My
For-

first __ love, __ you're ev-'ry breath that I take, __
ev-er, __ I'll hold you close in my arms, __

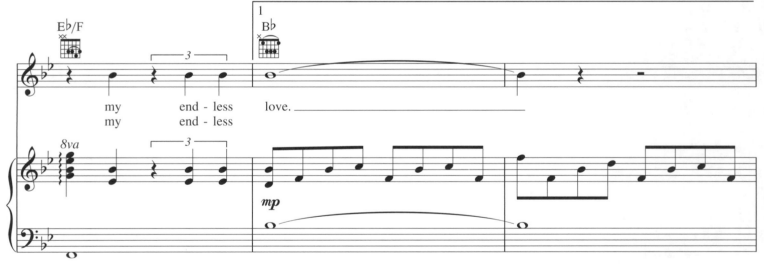

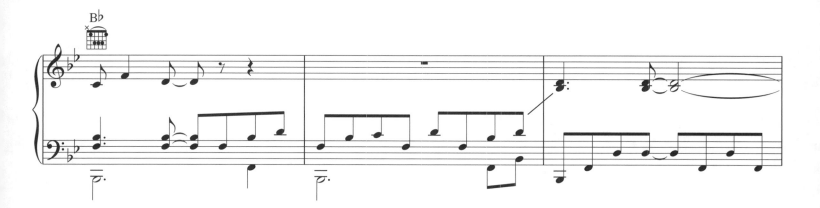

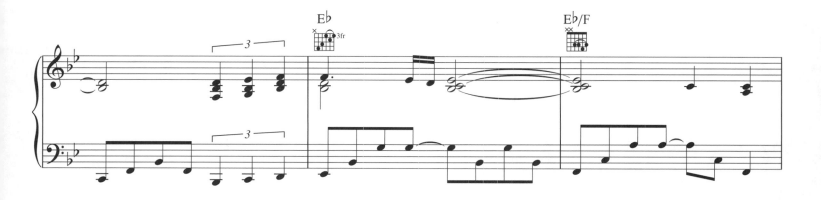

Oh, _____ and _____ love, _____

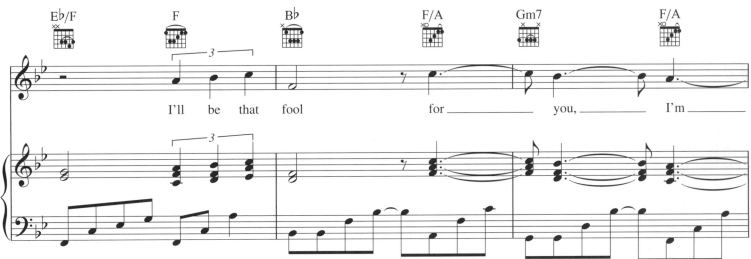

I'll be that fool for _____ you, _____ I'm _____

_____ sure; _____ you __ know I don't mind. _____

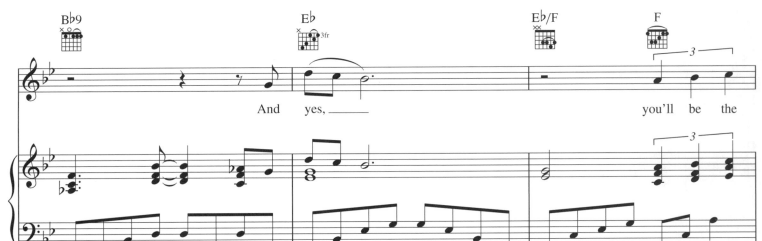

And yes, _____ you'll be the

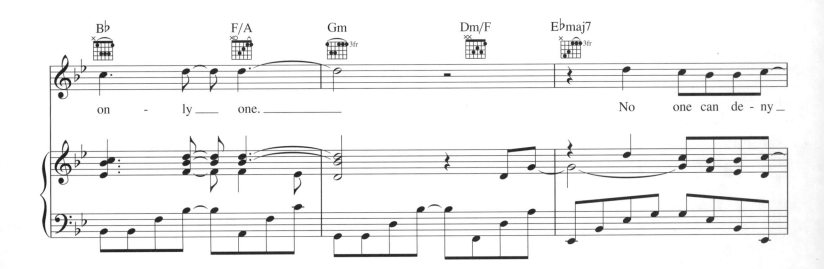

on - ly __ one. _____ No one can de - ny __

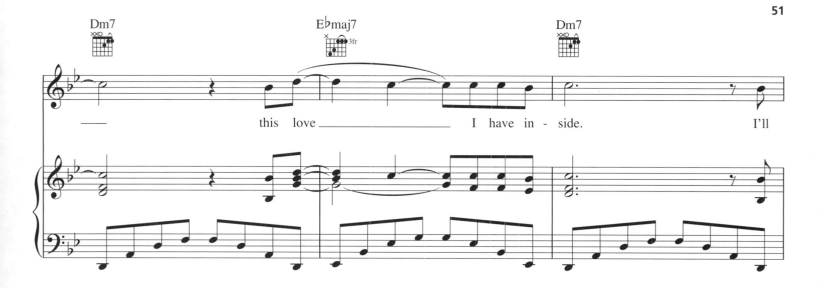

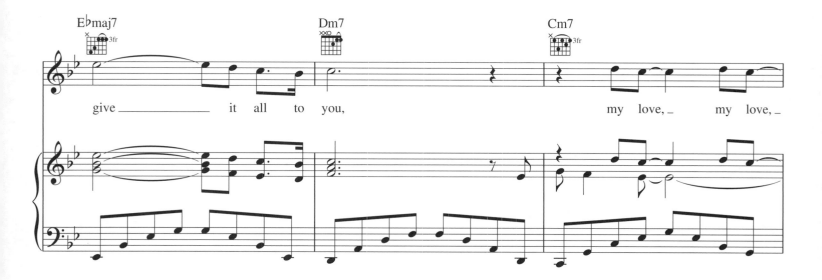

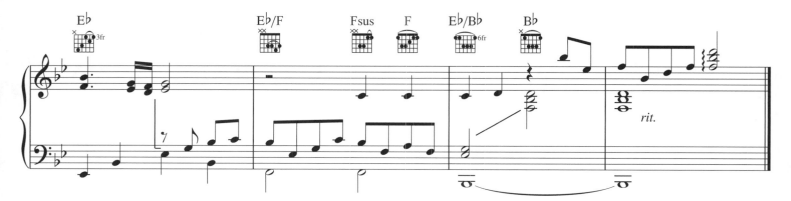

EXHALE
(Shoop Shoop)
from the Original Soundtrack Album WAITING TO EXHALE

Words and Music by
BABYFACE

Easy R&B Ballad

(1.) Ev - 'ry - one falls in love some - times. _____ Some - times it's
(2.,3.) laugh, some - times you'll cry. _____ Life nev - er

wrong _____ and some - times it's right. For ev - 'ry
tells __ us __ the whens or whys. When you've got

win some - one must fail, but there comes a
friends to wish you well, you'll find a

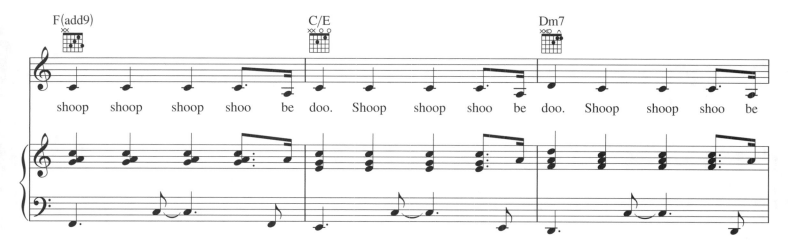

54

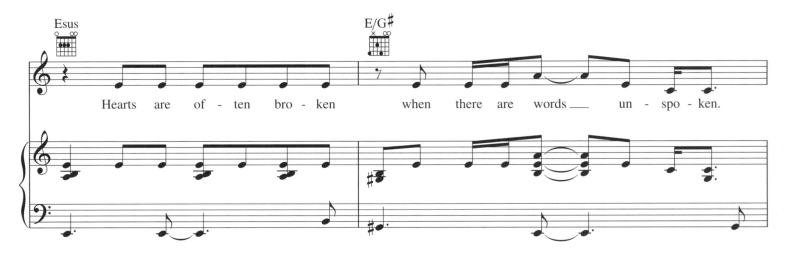

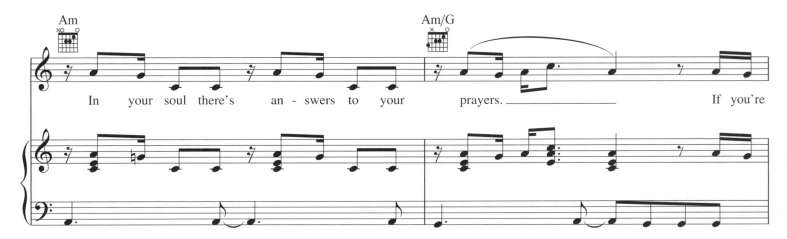

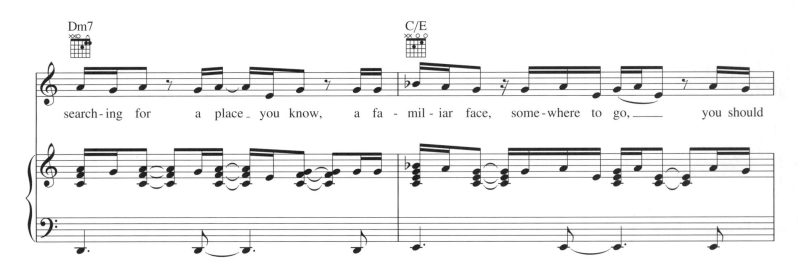

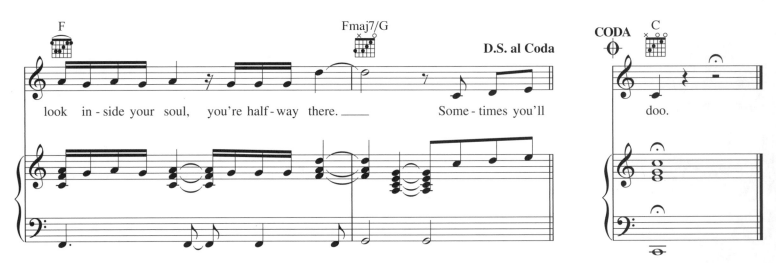

FOR ALL WE KNOW

from the Motion Picture LOVERS AND OTHER STRANGERS

Words by ROBB WILSON and ARTHUR JAMES
Music by FRED KARLIN

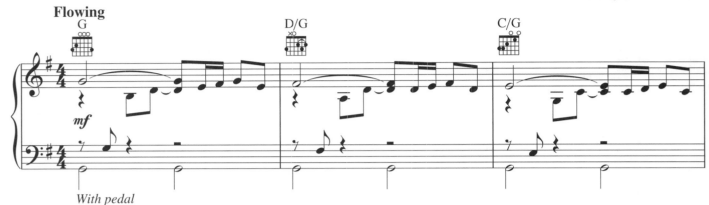

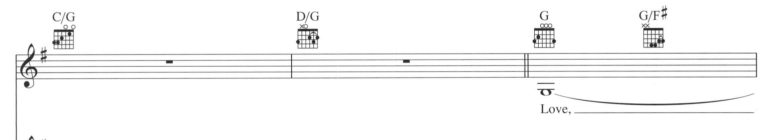

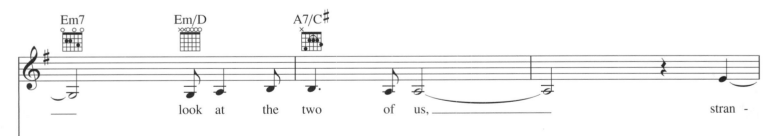

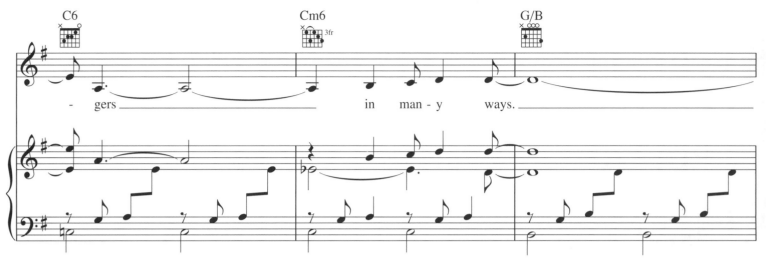

-gers _____ in man-y ways. _____

___ We've got a life - time ___ to

share, so much to say,

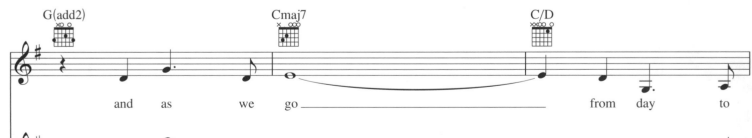

and as we go _____ from day to

day,

I'll feel you close to me,

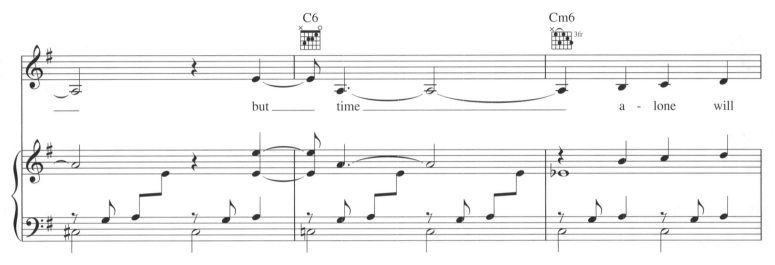

but _____ time _____ a - lone will

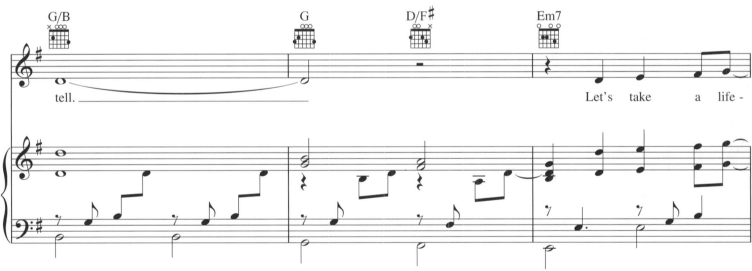

tell. _____ Let's take a life -

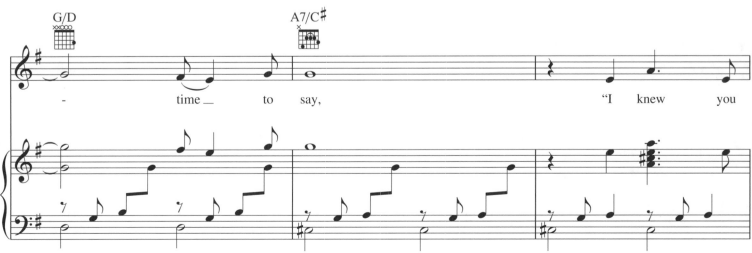

- time ___ to say, "I knew you

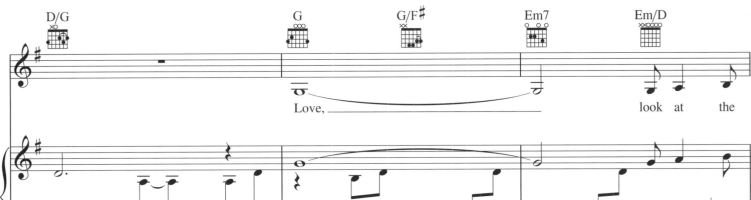

Love, _____ look at the

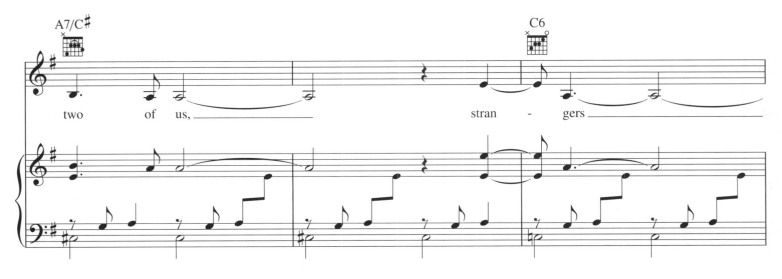

two of us, _____ stran - gers _____

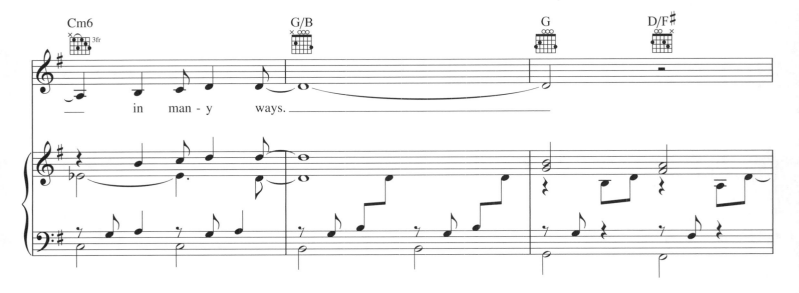

in man - y ways. _____

know. _____

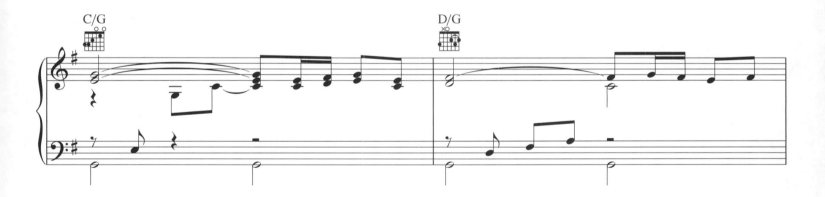

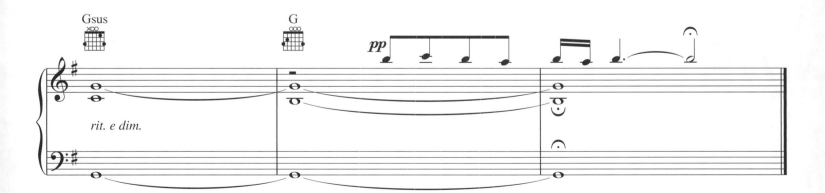

GLORY OF LOVE
Theme from KARATE KID PART II

Words and Music by DAVID FOSTER,
PETER CETERA and DIANE NINI

To-night _ it's ver-y clear, as we're both stand-ing here, _

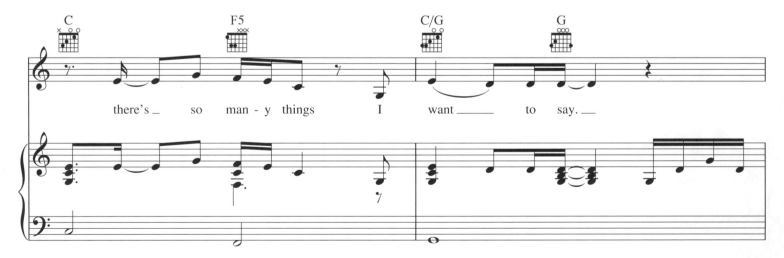

there's _ so man-y things I want _____ to say. _

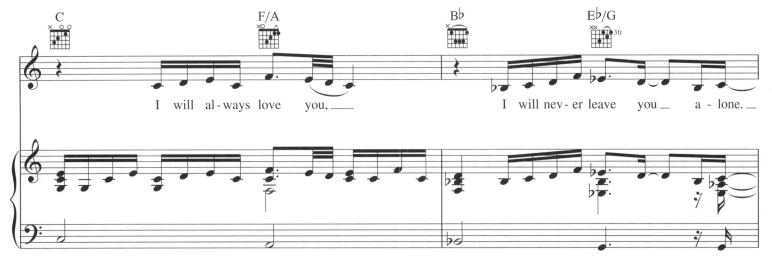

I will al-ways love you, ___ I will nev-er leave you ___ a - lone. ___

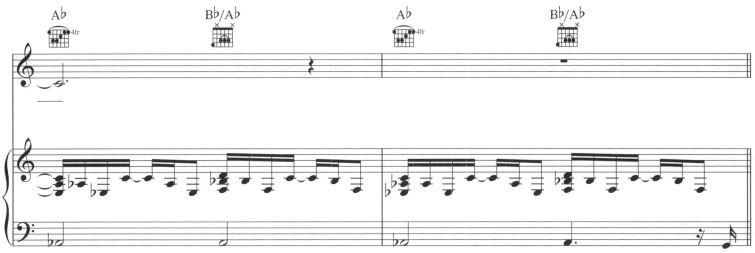

Some-times I just for - get, say things I might re - gret, ___
You keep me stand - ing tall, you help me through it all, ___

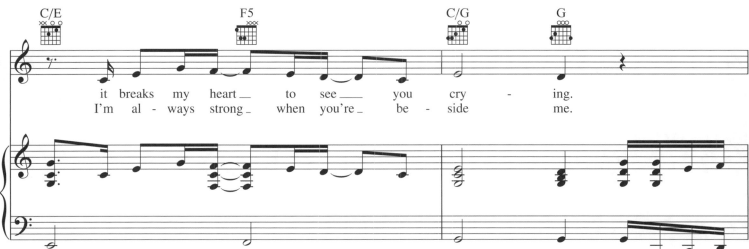

it breaks my heart ___ to see ___ you cry - ing.
I'm al - ways strong ___ when you're ___ be - side me.

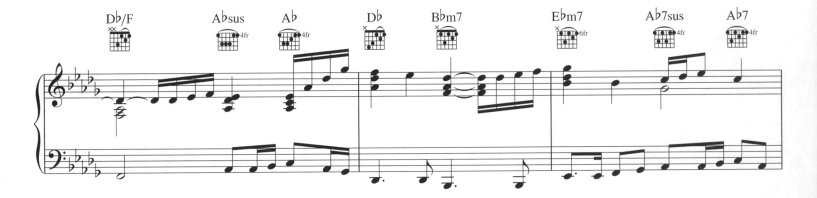

We'll live for-ev-er, know-ing to-geth-er that we did it all __ for the glo-

-ry of love. __ We did __ it all __ for love. __

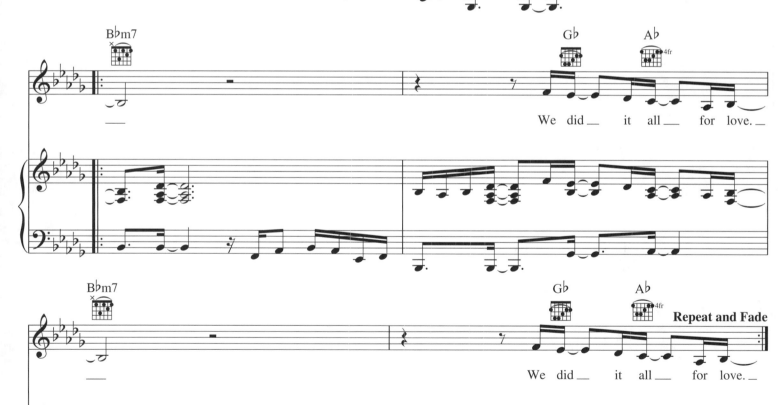

__ We did __ it all __ for love. __

Repeat and Fade

__ We did __ it all __ for love. __

HELLO AGAIN

from the Motion Picture THE JAZZ SINGER

Words by NEIL DIAMOND
Music by NEIL DIAMOND and ALAN LINDGREN

Moderately slow

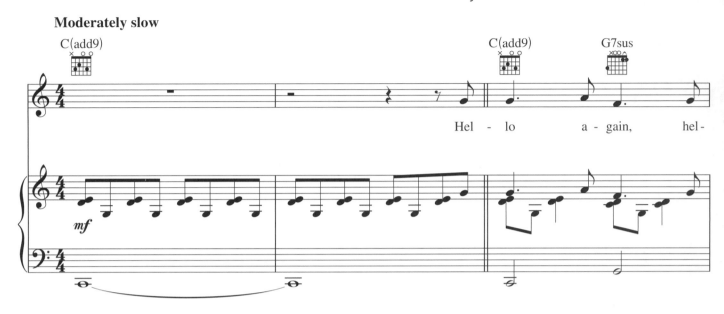

Hel - lo a - gain, hel-

lo. Just called to say 'hel - lo'. I

could - n't sleep at all to - night. And I know it's late, but I

could-n't wait.   Hel - lo,   my friend,   hel - lo.   Just

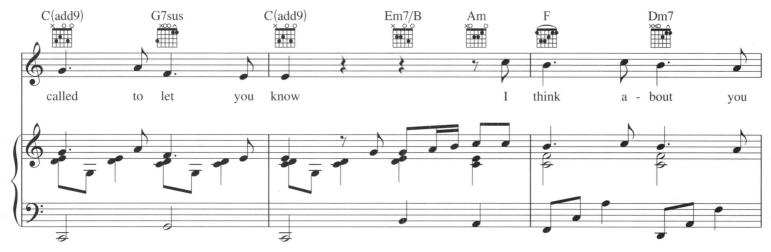

called   to let   you know   I think   a - bout   you

ev - 'ry night   when I'm here a - lone   and you're there at home.   Hel-

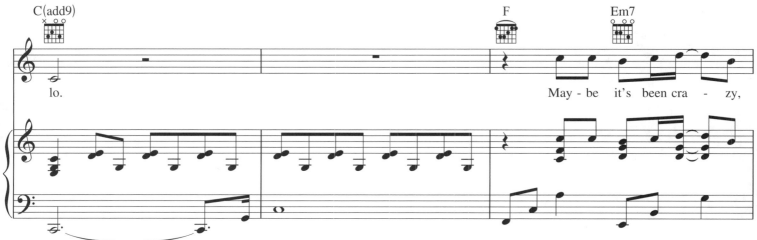

lo.   May - be it's been cra - zy,

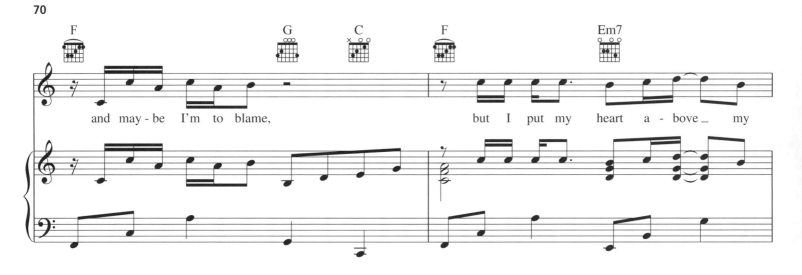

and may-be I'm to blame, but I put my heart a-bove _ my

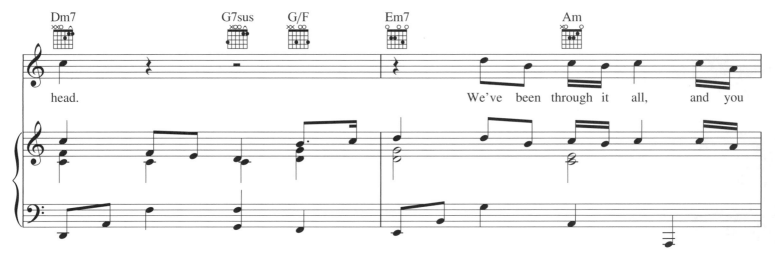

head. We've been through it all, and you

loved me just _ the same. _ And when you're not there, I

just need _ to hear: Hel-lo, my friend, hel-lo. It's

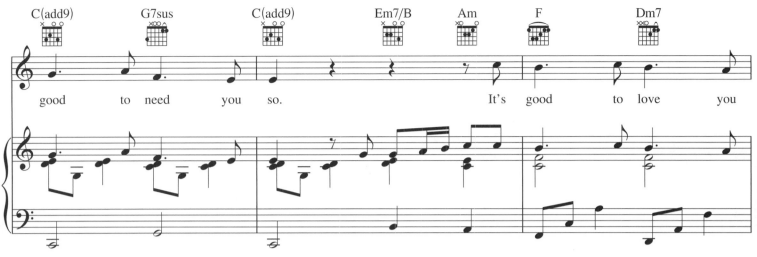

good to need you so. It's good to love you

like I do and to feel this way when I hear you say 'hel-

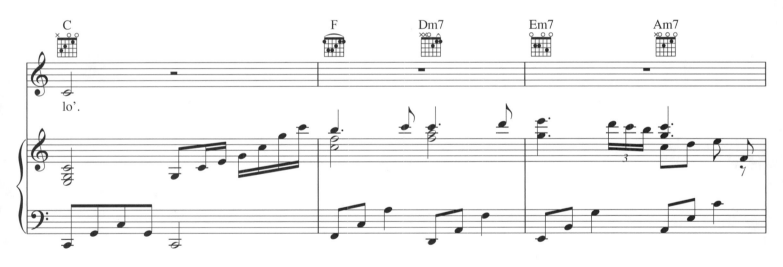

lo'.

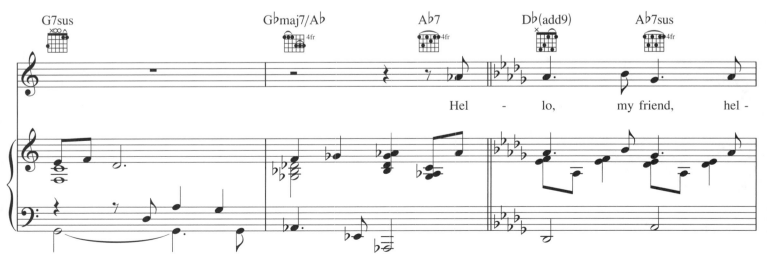

Hel - lo, my friend, hel-

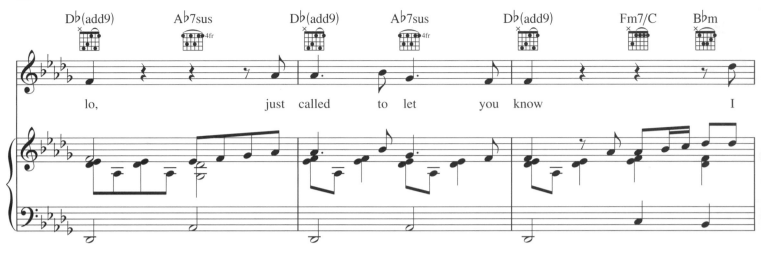

lo, just called to let you know I

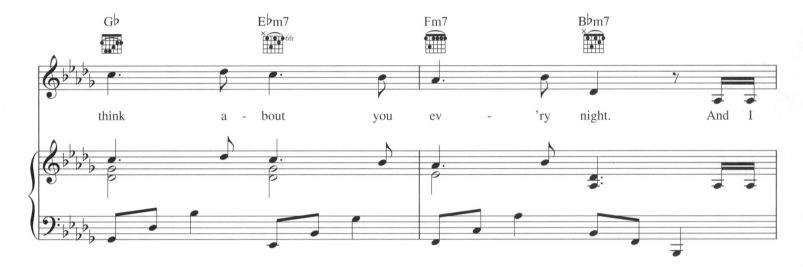

think a - bout you ev - 'ry night. And I

know it's late, but I could -n't wait. Hel -

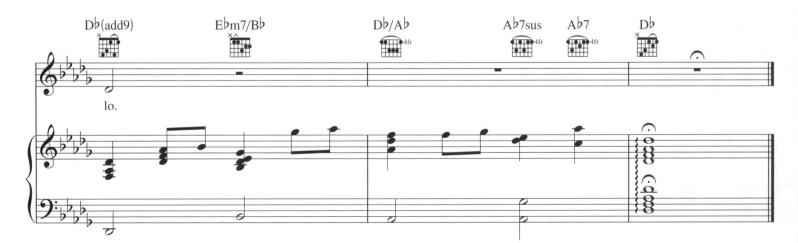

lo.

HOPELESSLY DEVOTED TO YOU

from GREASE

Words and Music by
JOHN FARRAR

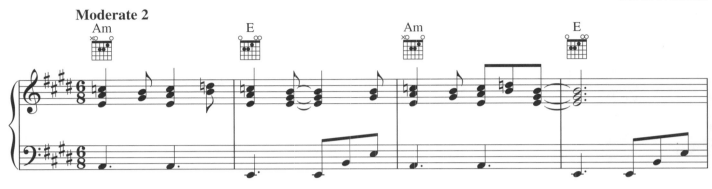

Moderate 2

Guess

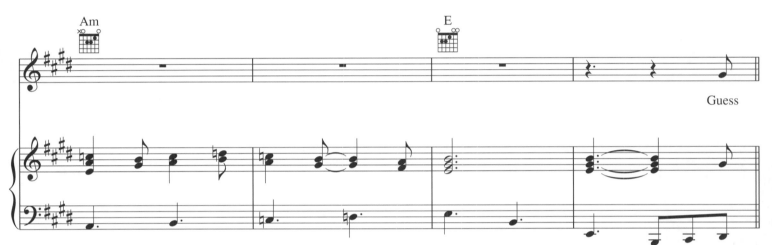

mine is not the first _____ heart bro - ken, _____ my
know I'm just a fool _____ who's will - in' _____ to
head is say - in', "Fool, _____ for - get him." _____ My

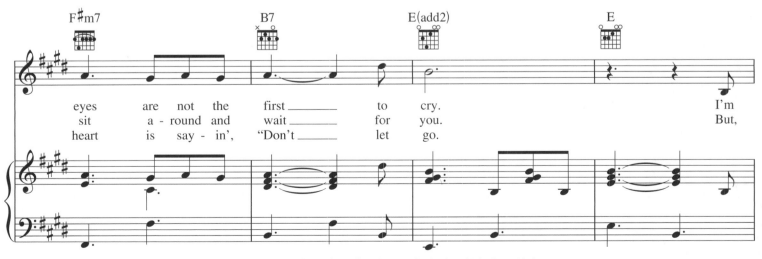

eyes are not the first _____ to cry. I'm
sit a - round and wait _____ for you. But,
heart is say - in', "Don't _____ let go.

not the ___ first to know   there's just no ___ get - tin' o - ver
ba - by, ___ can't you see   there's noth - in' ___ else for me ___ to
Hold on ___ to the end." And that's what ___ I in - tend ___ to

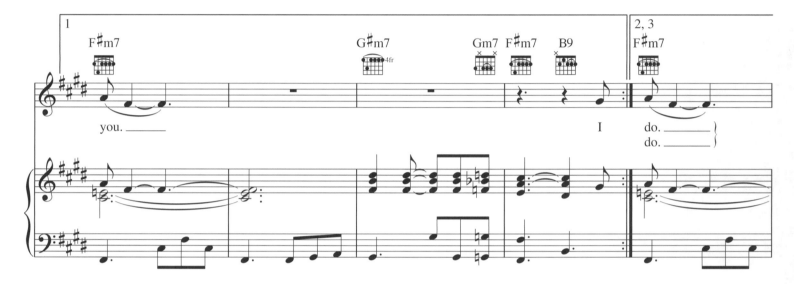

you. ___   I   do. ___
                                                     do. ___

I'm hope - less - ly de - vot - ed ___ to you.

But   now   there's   no - where to   hide ___ since you

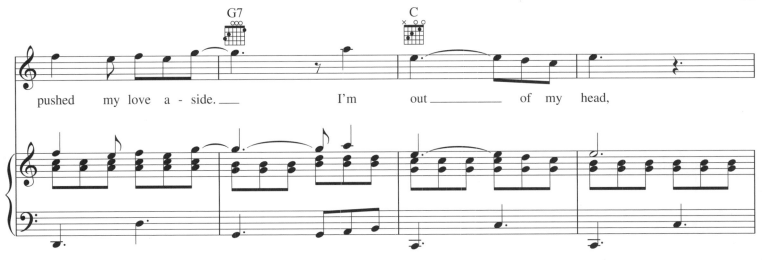

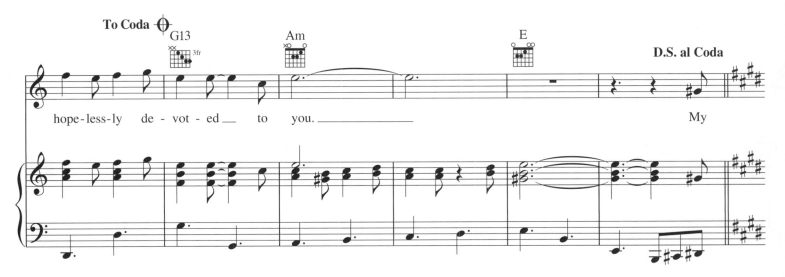

HOW DEEP IS YOUR LOVE

from the Motion Picture SATURDAY NIGHT FEVER

Words and Music by BARRY GIBB,
ROBIN GIBB and MAURICE GIBB

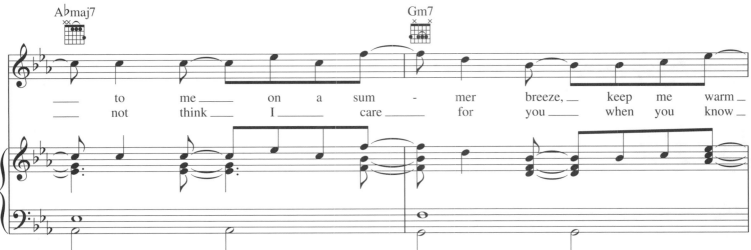

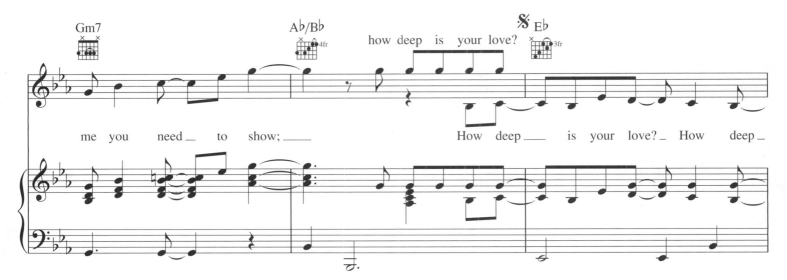

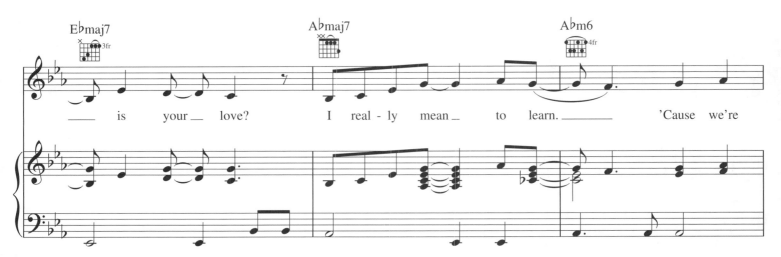

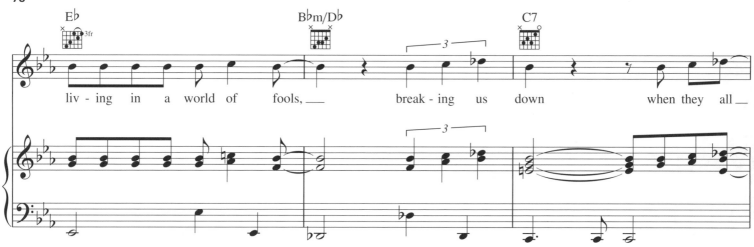

living in a world of fools, ___ break-ing us down when they all ___

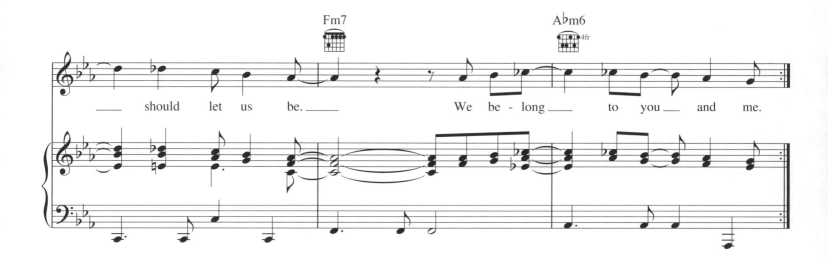

___ should let us be. ___ We be-long ___ to you ___ and me.

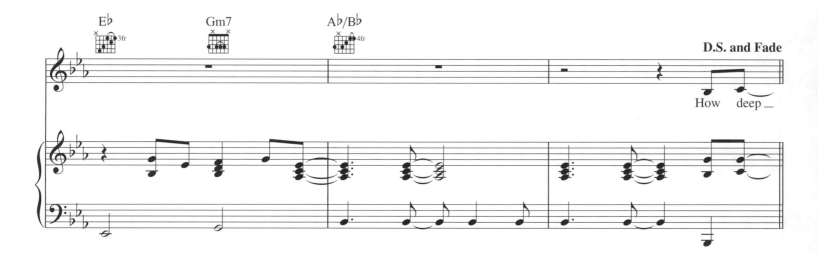

D.S. and Fade

How deep ___

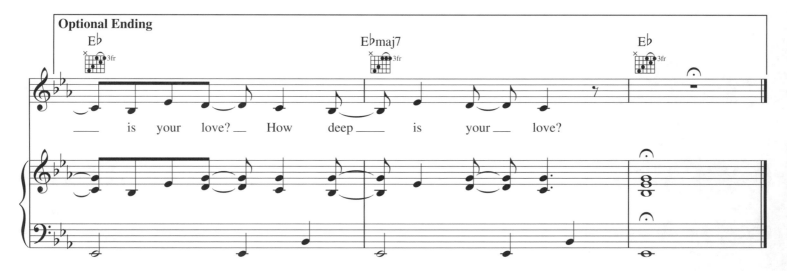

Optional Ending

___ is your love? ___ How deep ___ is your ___ love?

I FINALLY FOUND SOMEONE

from THE MIRROR HAS TWO FACES

Words and Music by BARBRA STREISAND,
MARVIN HAMLISCH, R.J. LANGE
and BRYAN ADAMS

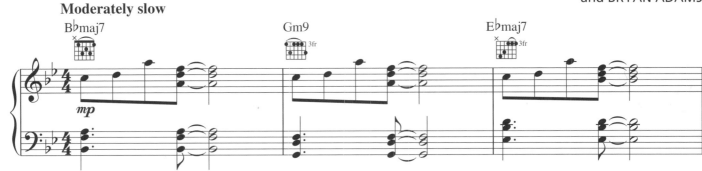

Male: I fi-n'lly found some-one who knocks me off my feet.

I fi-n'lly found the one __ that makes me feel com-plete.

Female: It start-ed o-ver cof-fee. We start-ed out as friends.

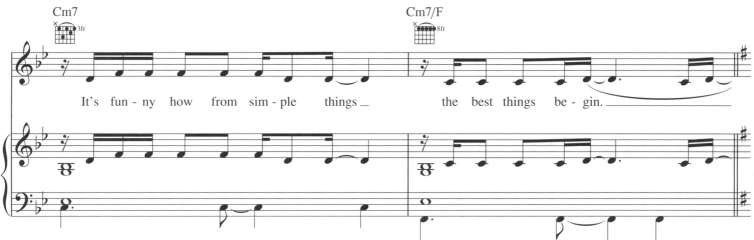

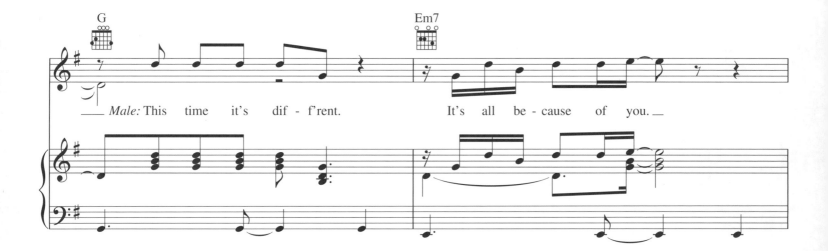

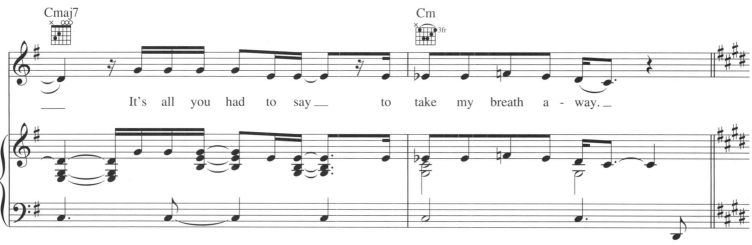

It's all you had to say __ to take my breath a - way. __

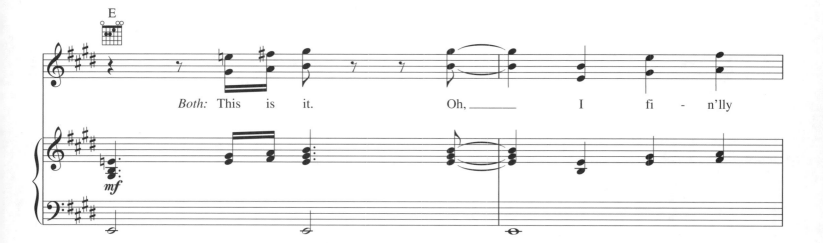

Both: This is it. Oh, _____ I fi - n'lly

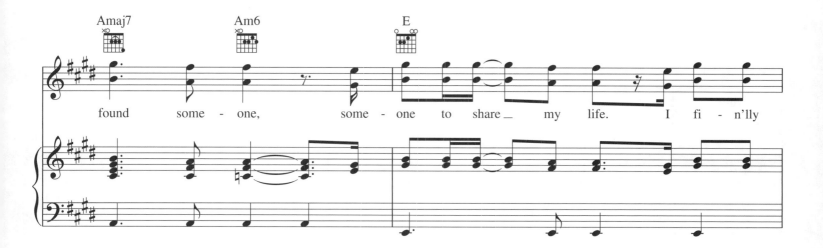

found some - one, some - one to share __ my life. I fi - n'lly

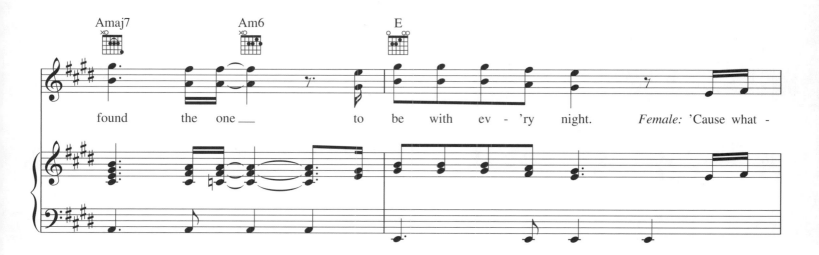

found the one __ to be with ev - 'ry night. *Female:* 'Cause what -

ev - er I do, ___ *Male:* it's just got to be you. ___ *Both:* My

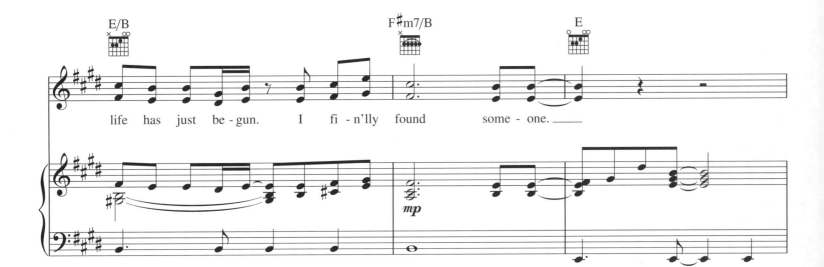

life has just be - gun. I fi - n'lly found some - one. ___

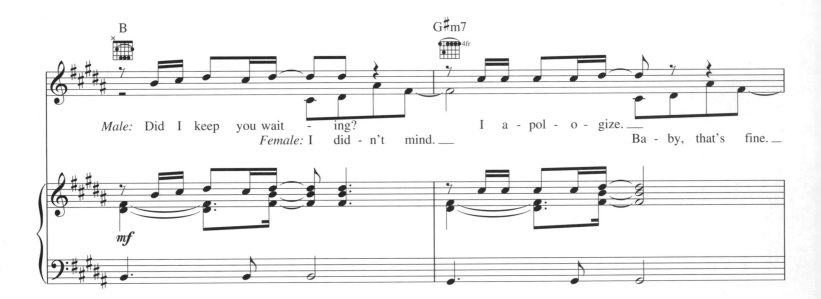

Male: Did I keep you wait - ing? I a - pol - o - gize. *Female:* I did - n't mind. ___ Ba - by, that's fine. ___

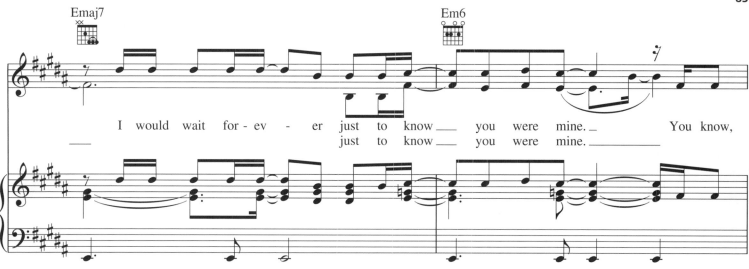

I would wait for - ev - er just to know___ you were mine.___ You know,
___ just to know___ you were mine.___

I love your hair.___ I love what you wear.
Are you sure it looks right?___ Is - n't it too tight?___

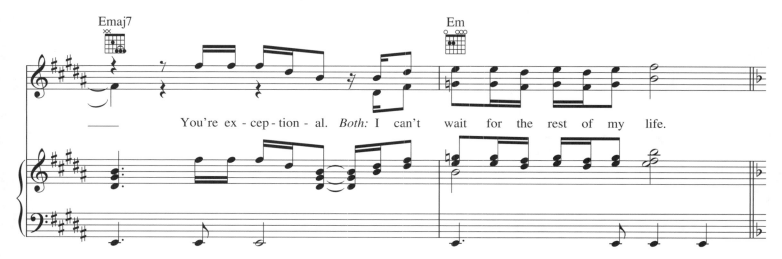

___ You're ex - cep - tion - al. *Both:* I can't wait for the rest of my life.

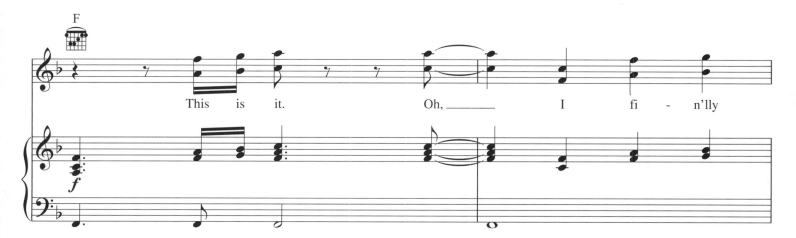

This is it. Oh,___ I fi - n'lly

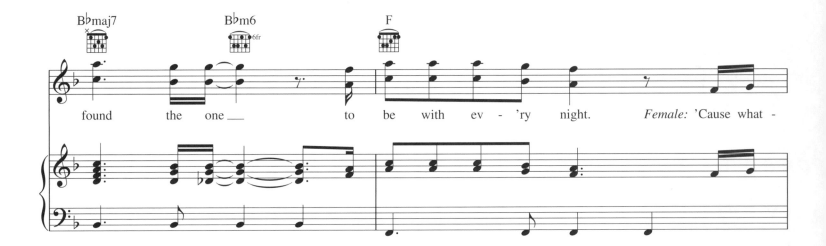

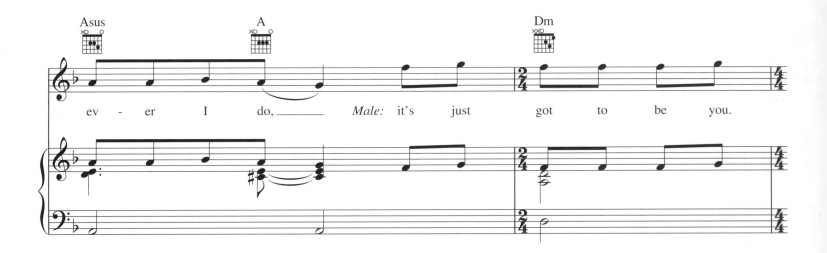

I HAVE NOTHING

from THE BODYGUARD

Words and Music by DAVID FOSTER
and LINDA THOMPSON-JENNER

Moderately, with "2" feel

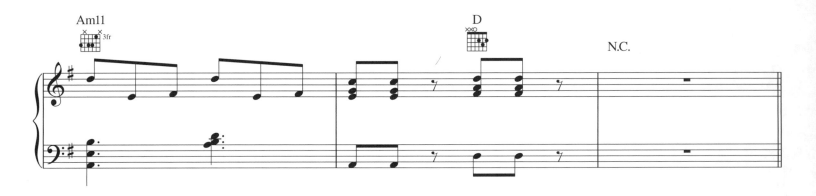

Share my life, take me from what I am. 'Cause
You see through, right to the heart of me.   You

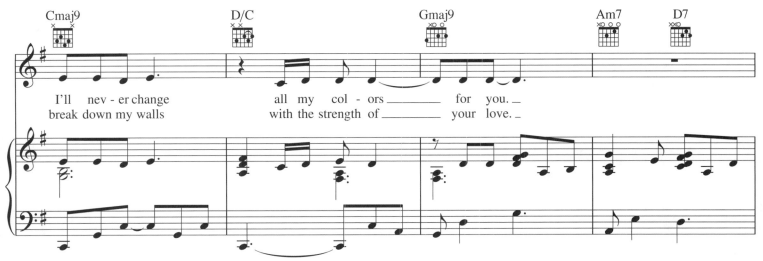

I'll nev - er change all my col - ors _____ for you. _
break down my walls with the strength of _____ your love. _

Take my love, I'll nev - er ask for too much just
I nev - er knew love like I've known it with you. Will a

all that you _ are and ev - 'ry - thing that you do. }
mem - ory sur - vive, one I can hold on to? }

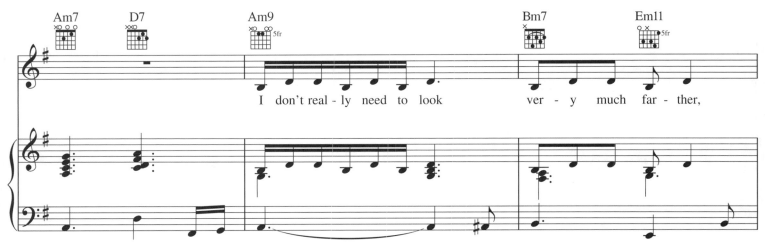

I don't real - ly need to look ver - y much far - ther,

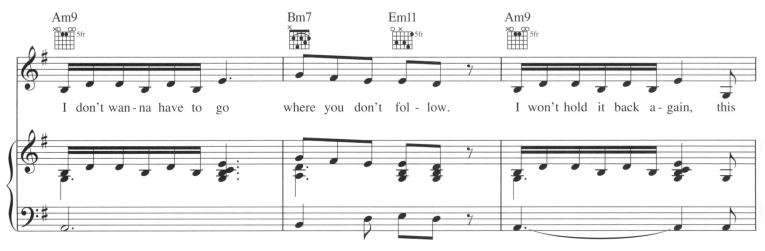

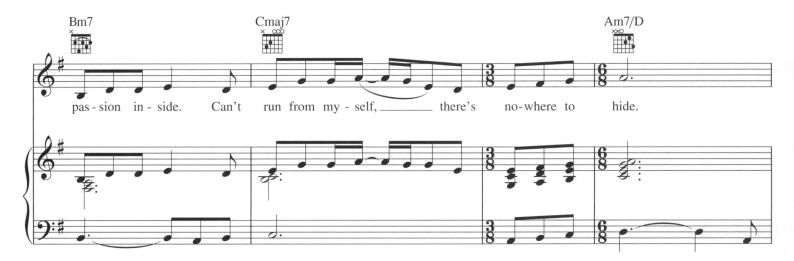

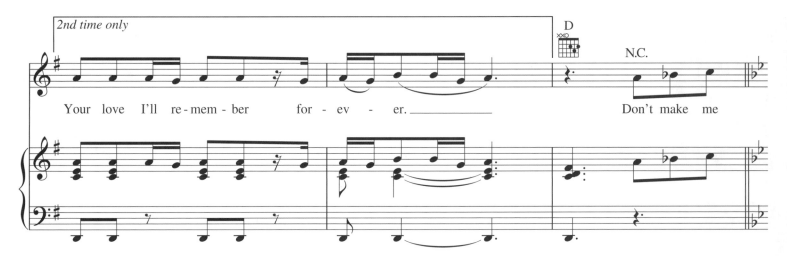

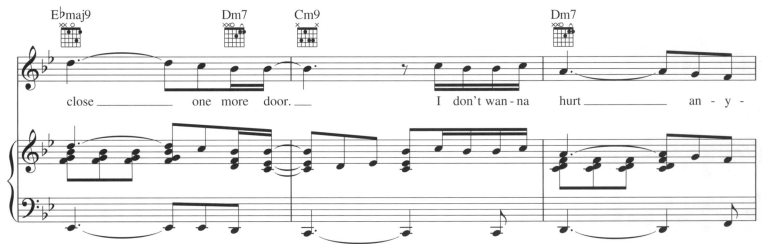

more. Stay in my arms _____ if you dare, ____ or must I i-mag - ine you

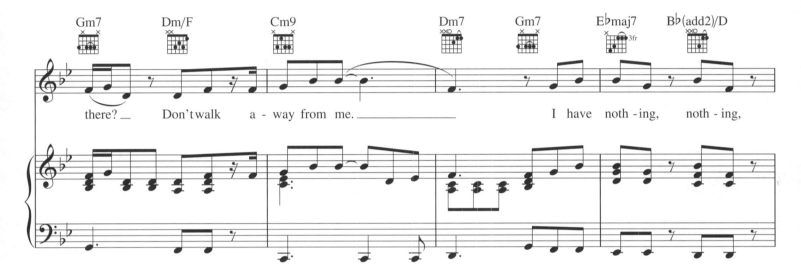

there? __ Don't walk a - way from me. _____ I have noth -ing, noth -ing,

noth - ing if I don't have you, _____ you, _____

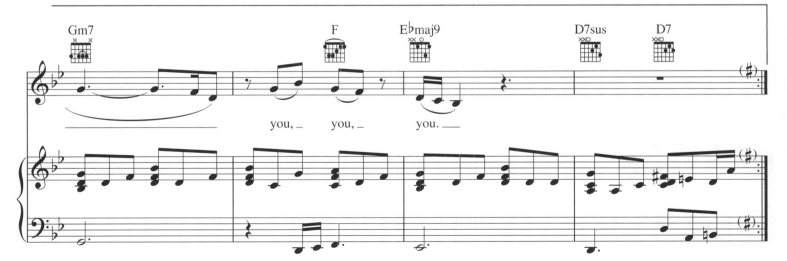

you, _ you, _ you. ____

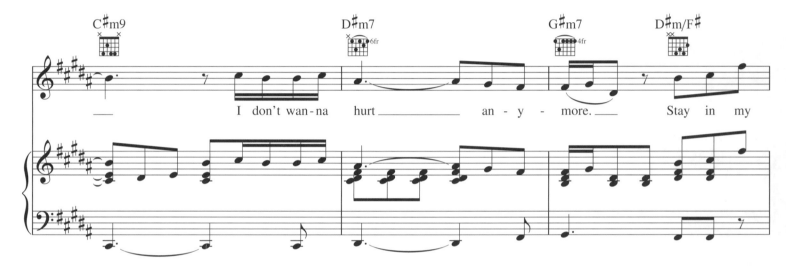

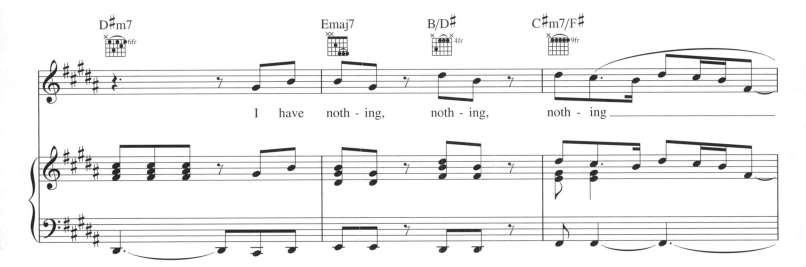

I JUST CALLED TO SAY I LOVE YOU

featured in THE WOMAN IN RED

Words and Music by
STEVIE WONDER

1. No New Year's Day   to cel - e -
2. rain;   no flow - ers

3., 4. *(See additional lyrics)*

brate;   no choc - 'late - cov - ered can - dy hearts
bloom;   no wed - ding Sat - ur - day   with - in

to give   a - way.   No first   of
the month   of   June.   But what   it

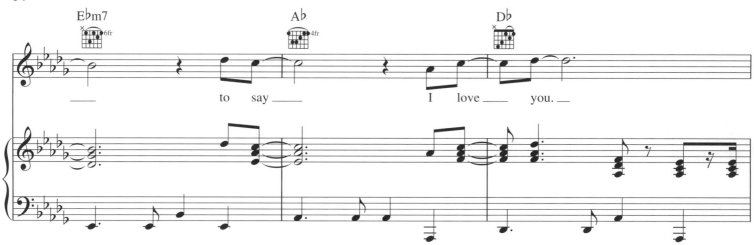

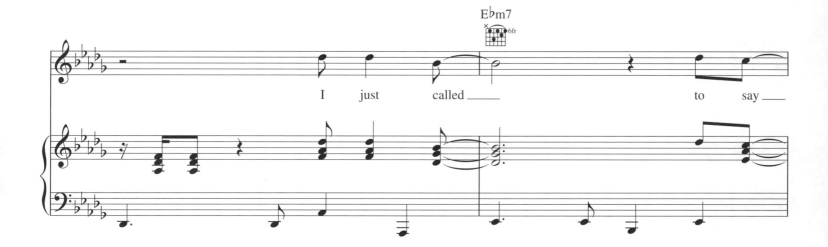

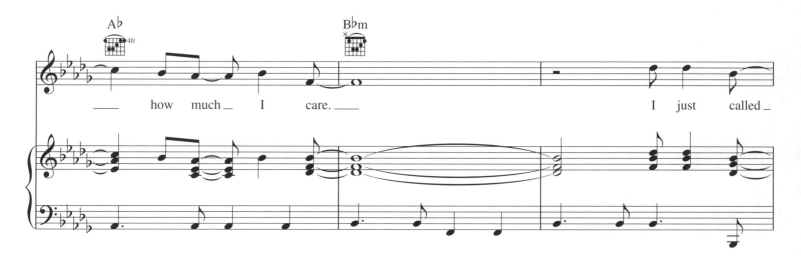

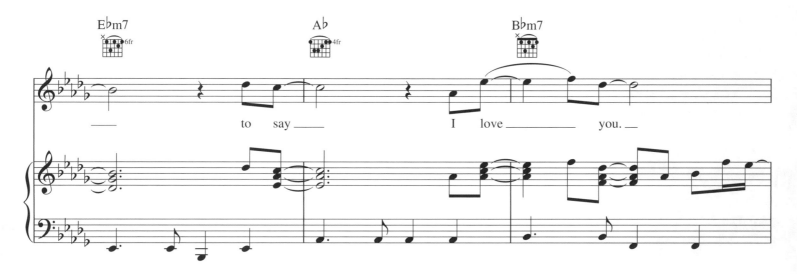

And I mean ___ it from ___ the bot -

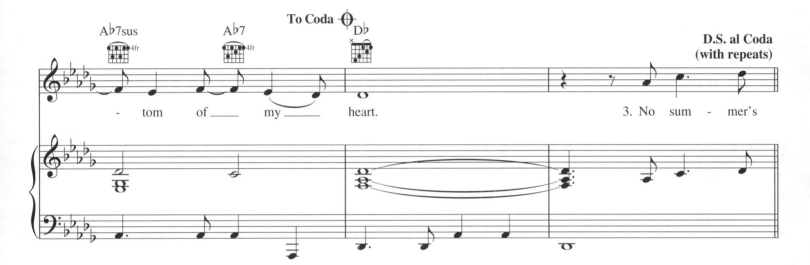

- tom of ___ my ___ heart.   3. No sum - mer's

To Coda   **D.S. al Coda**
(with repeats)

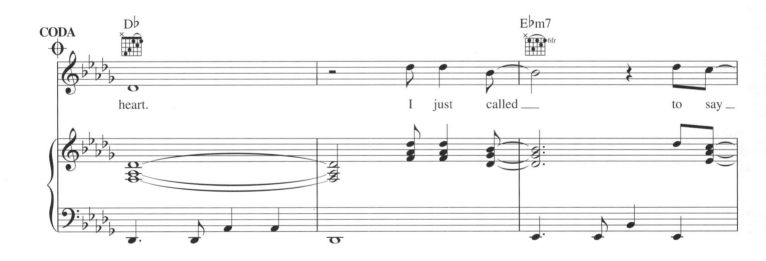

CODA

heart.   I just called ___ to say ___

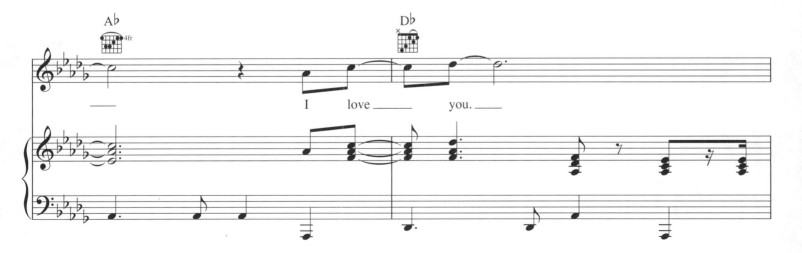

___ I love ___ you. ___

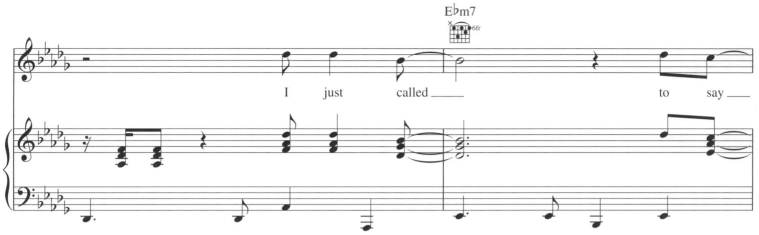

I just called _____ to say _____

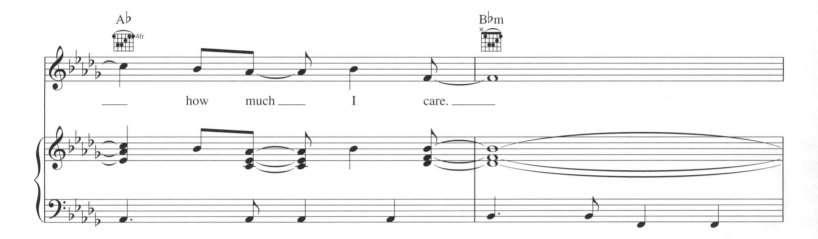

_____ how much _____ I care. _____

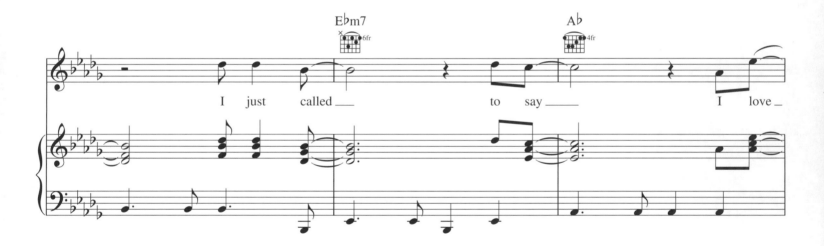

I just called _____ to say _____ I love _

_____ you. _ And I mean _____ it from _____ the bot -

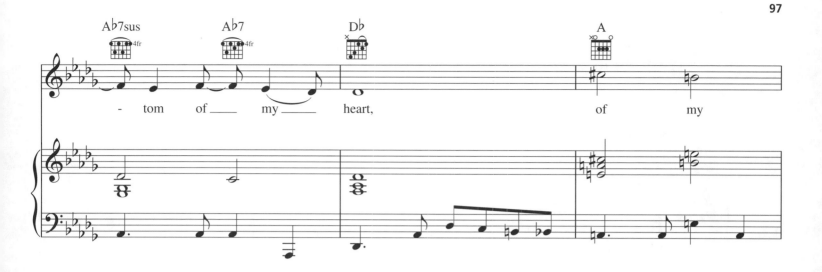

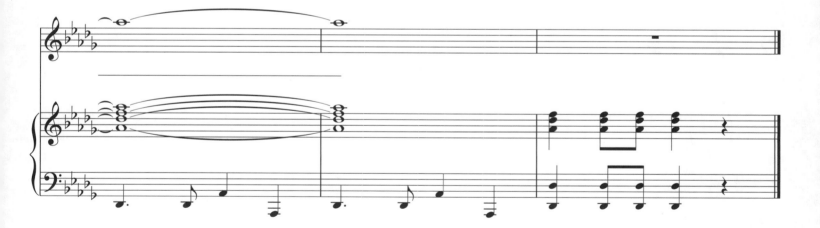

Additional Lyrics

3. No summer's high; no warm July;
   No harvest moon to light one tender August night.
   No autumn breeze; no falling leaves;
   Not even time for birds to fly to southern skies.

4. No Libra sun; no Halloween;
   No giving thanks to all the Christmas joy you bring.
   But what it is, though old so new
   To fill your heart like no three words could ever do.
   Chorus

I SAY A LITTLE PRAYER

featured in the TriStar Motion Picture MY BEST FRIEND'S WEDDING

Lyric by HAL DAVID
Music by BURT BACHARACH

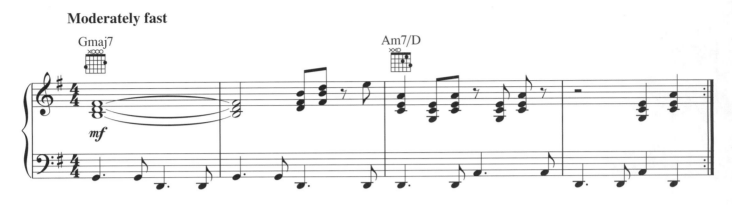

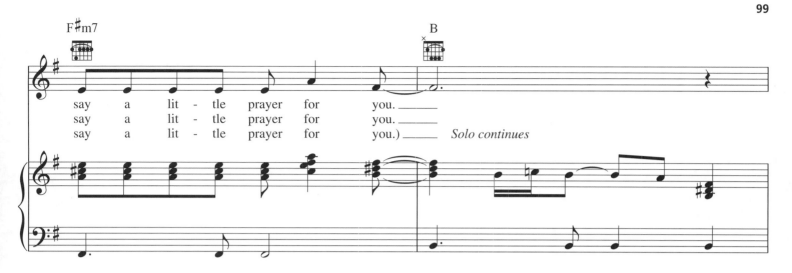

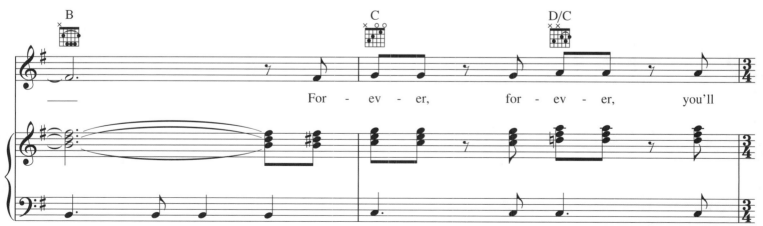

stay in my heart __ and I will love you. For - ev - er and ev - er, we

nev - er will part. __ Oh, how I'll love you. To - geth - er, to - geth - er, that's

how it must be. __ To live with - out you would on - ly mean heart - break for

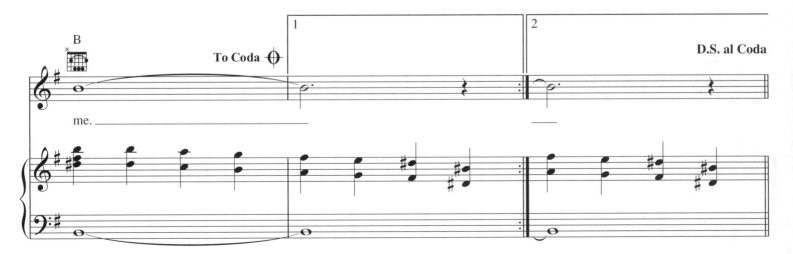

me. ___

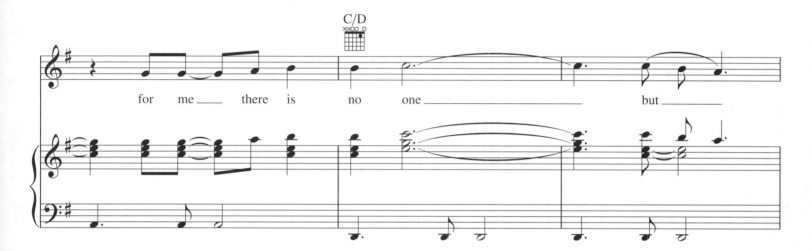

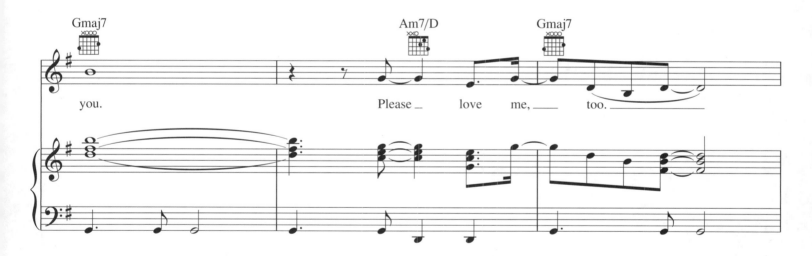

prayer. Say ___ you love me, too. ___

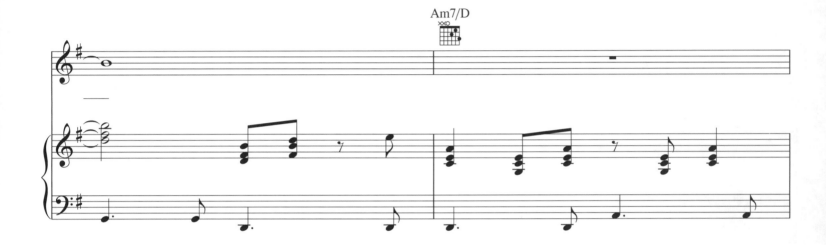

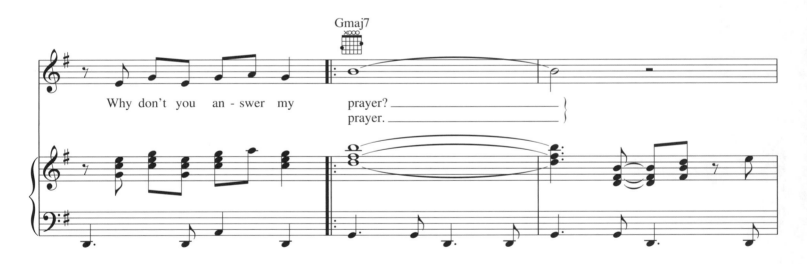

Why don't you an- swer my prayer? ___
prayer. ___

You know, ev- 'ry day I say a lit- tle

Repeat and Fade

I WILL ALWAYS LOVE YOU

from THE BODYGUARD

Words and Music by
DOLLY PARTON

will_ al - ways_ love_ you._ I_

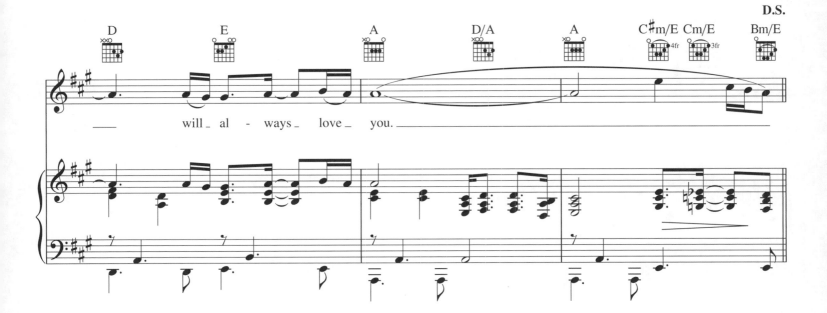

D.S.

will_ al - ways_ love_ you._

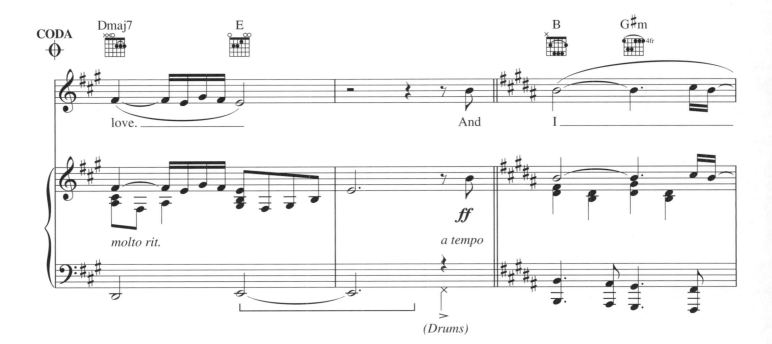

CODA

love._ And I_

molto rit.

ff

a tempo

(Drums)

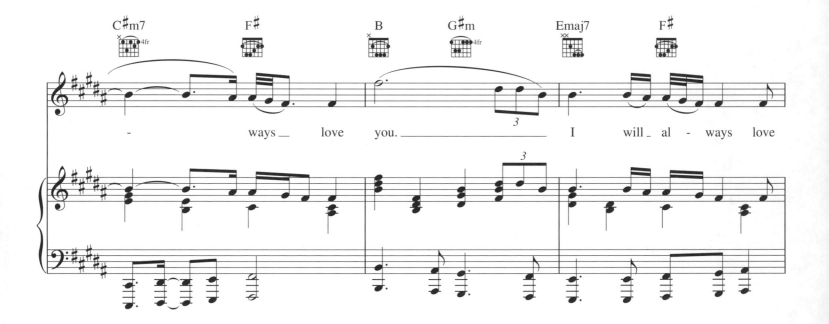

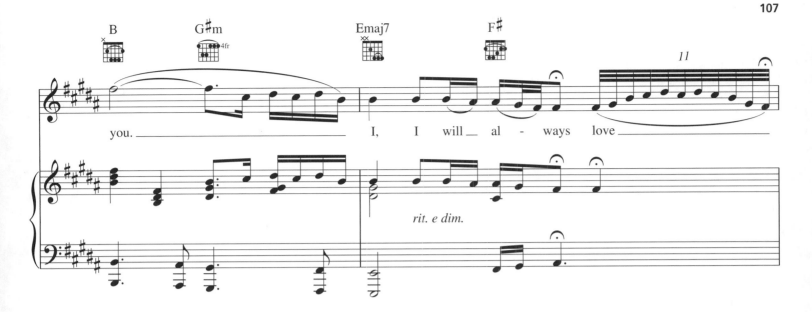

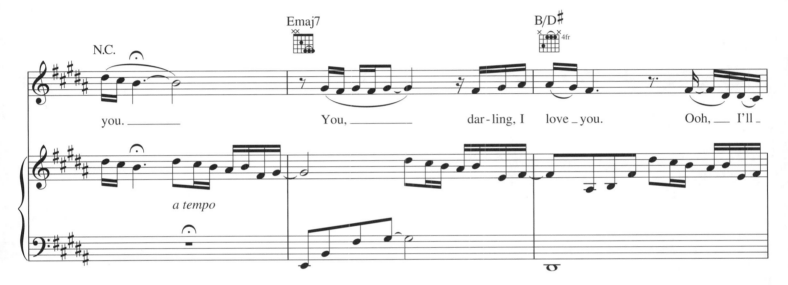

Additional Lyrics

3. I hope life treats you kind.
   And I hope you have all you've dreamed of.
   And I wish to you, joy and happiness.
   But above all this, I wish you love.

I WILL REMEMBER YOU

Theme from THE BROTHERS McMULLEN

Words and Music by SARAH McLACHLAN,
SEAMUS EGAN and DAVE MERENDA

Moderately slow

I will re - mem - ber _____ you. _____

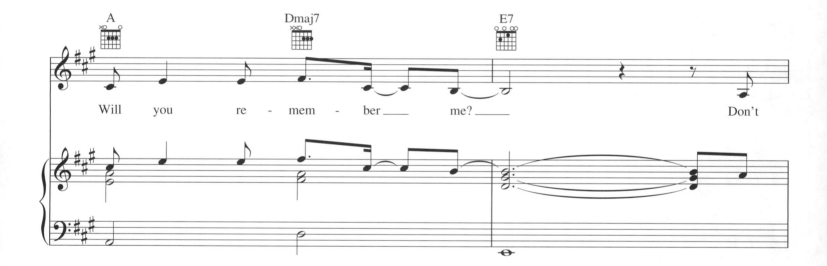

Will you re - mem - ber _____ me? _____ Don't

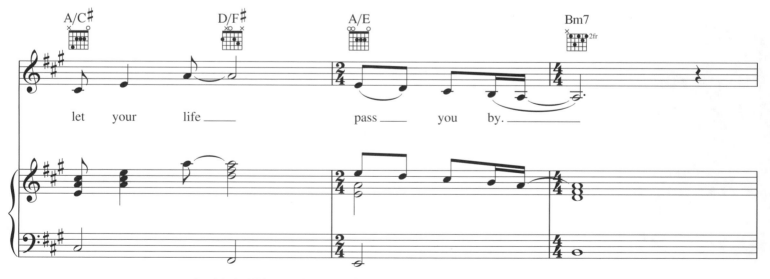

let your life _____ pass _____ you by. _____

your warmth up-on ___ me. I wan-na be the one. ___
ing in - side or we ___ can't be heard.
gave me ev-'ry-thing you had, oh, you gave me light. ___

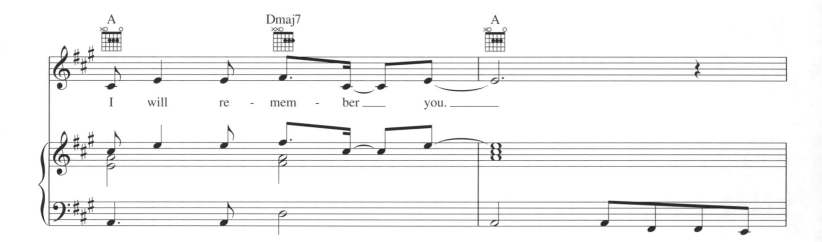

I will re - mem - ber ___ you. _____

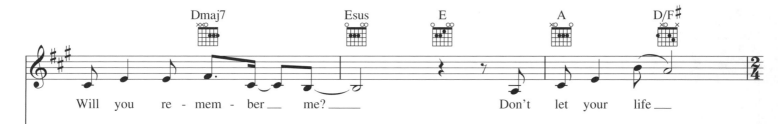

Will you re - mem - ber ___ me? _____ Don't let your life ___

pass ___ you by. _____ Weep not for _____ the

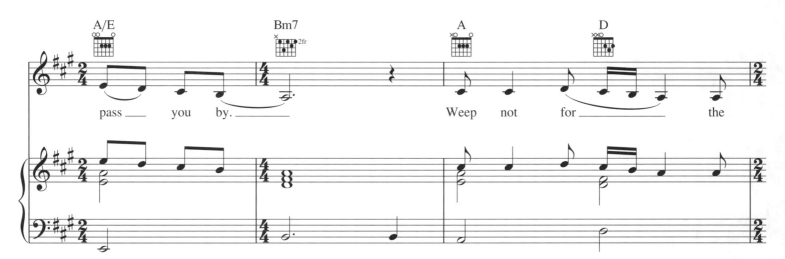

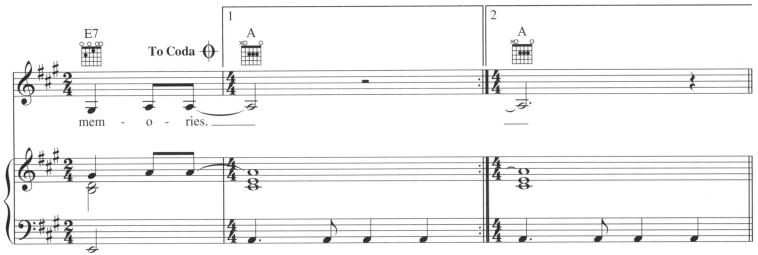

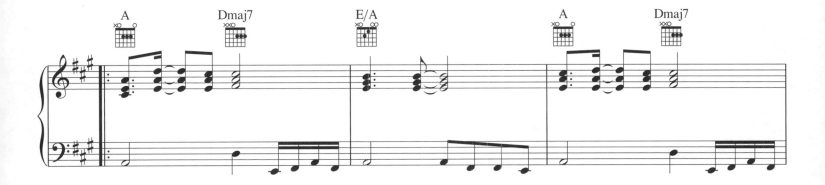

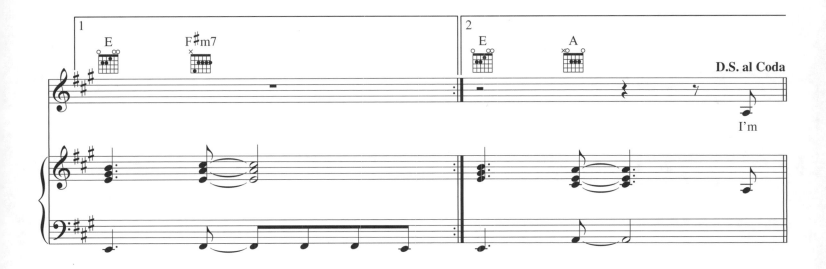

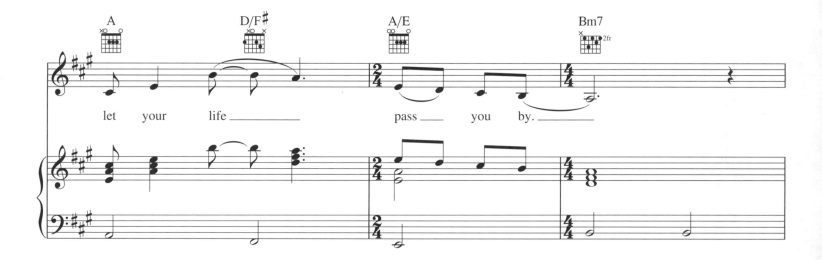

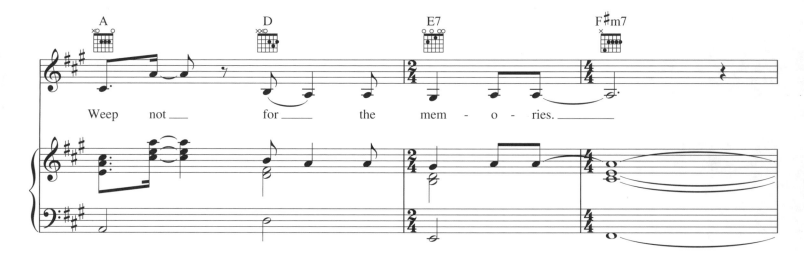

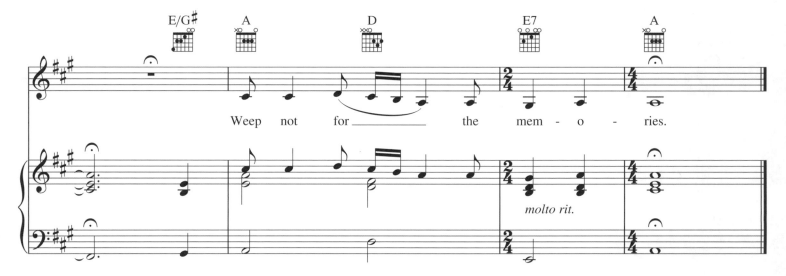

IT'S TIME TO SAY I LOVE YOU

Love Theme from THE OTHER SIDE OF THE MOUNTAIN–PART 2

Words and Music by LEE HOLDRIDGE
and MOLLY LEIKIN

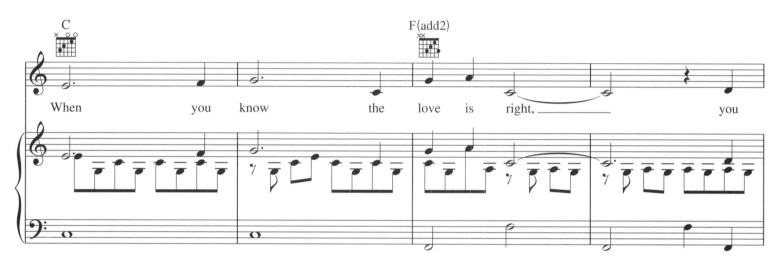

When you know the love is right, you gath - er dream bou - quets. And one or two will drift a - long wth you through

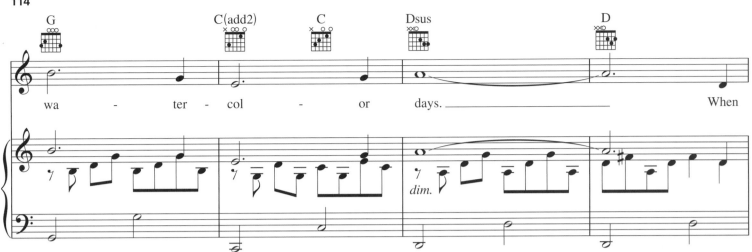

wa - ter - col - or days. _____ When

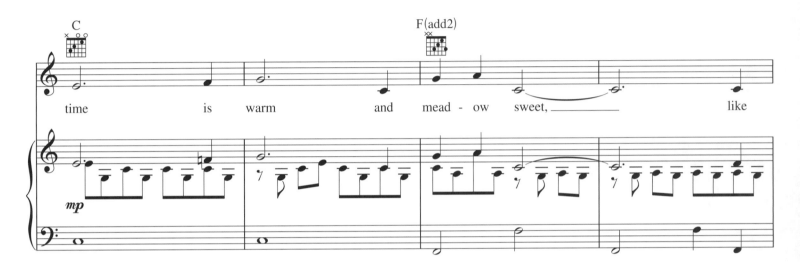

time   is   warm   and   mead - ow   sweet, _____ like

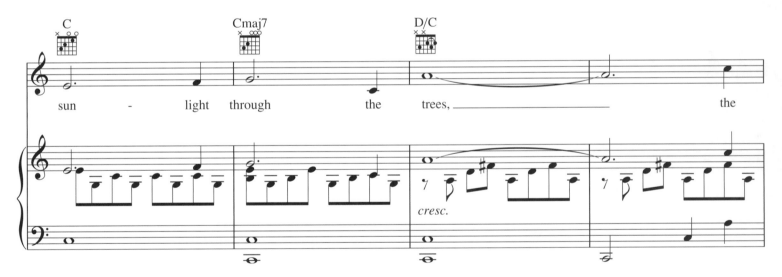

sun - light through   the   trees, _____ the

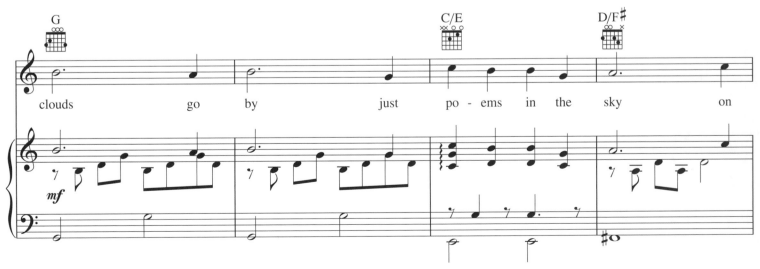

clouds   go   by   just   po - ems   in   the   sky   on

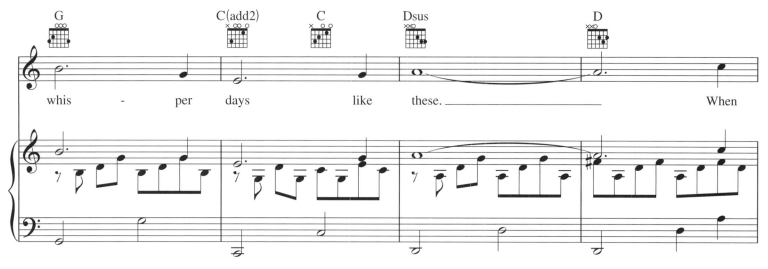

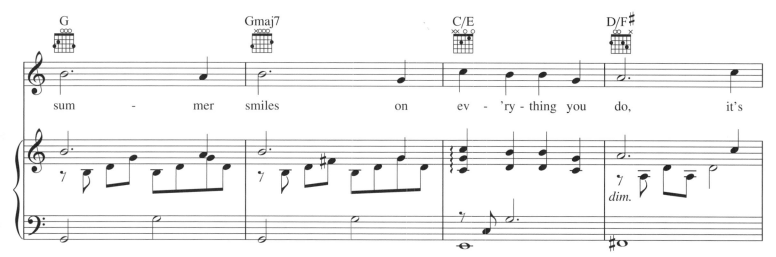

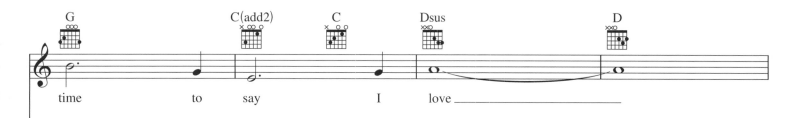

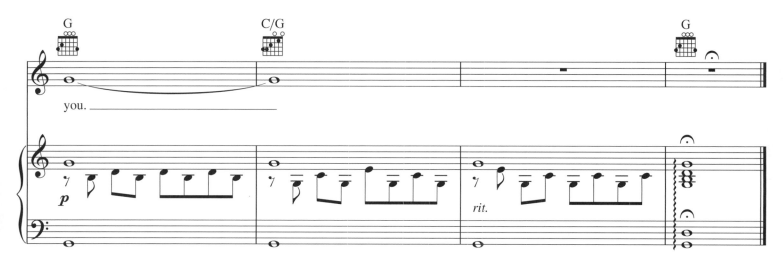

I WILL WAIT FOR YOU

from THE UMBRELLAS OF CHERBOURG

Music by MICHEL LEGRAND
Original French Text by JACQUES DEMY
English Words by NORMAN GIMBEL

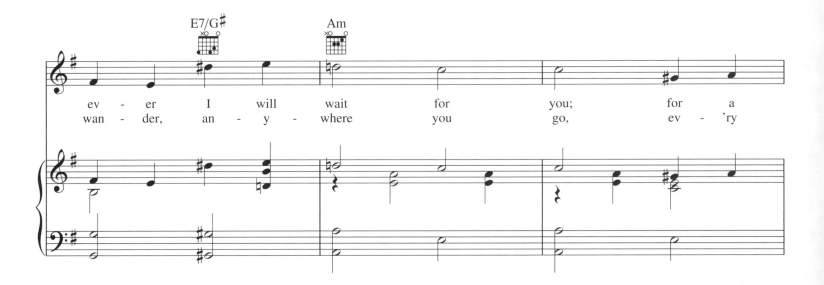

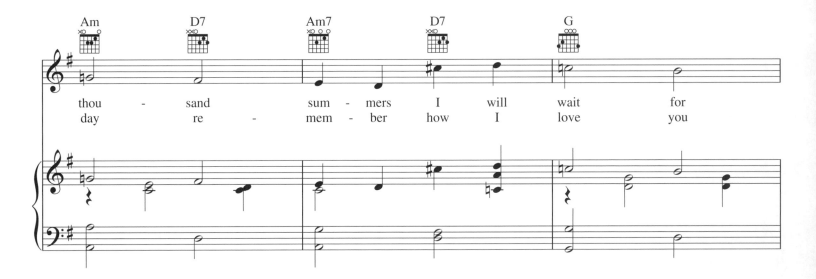

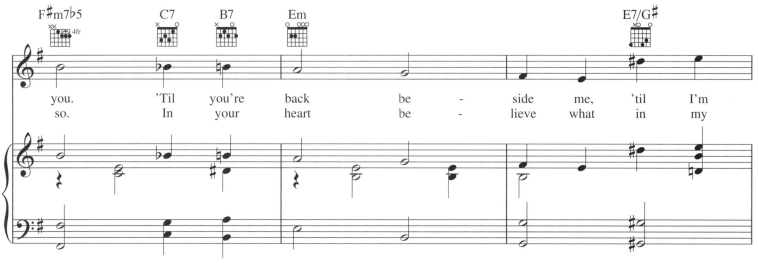

you. 'Til you're back be - side me, 'til I'm
so. In your heart be - lieve what in my

hold - ing you, 'til I hear you sigh
heart I know, that for - ev - er - more

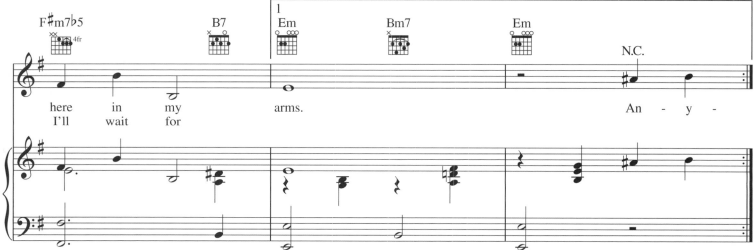

here in my arms. An - y -
I'll wait for

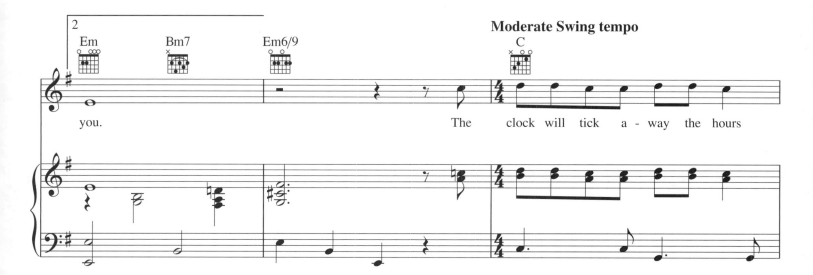

you.

Moderate Swing tempo

The clock will tick a - way the hours

one by one ___ and then the time will come when all the wait-ing's done, ___ the

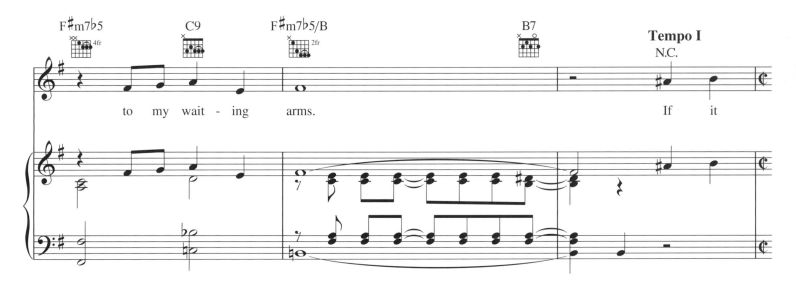

time when you re-turn and find me here and run ___ straight

to my wait-ing arms. If it

takes for - ev - er I will wait for

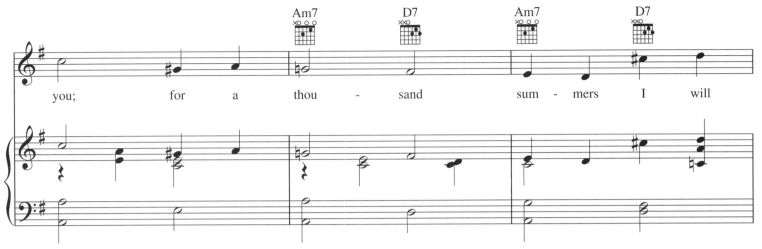

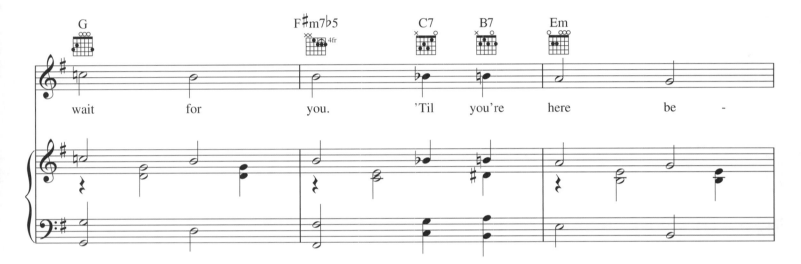

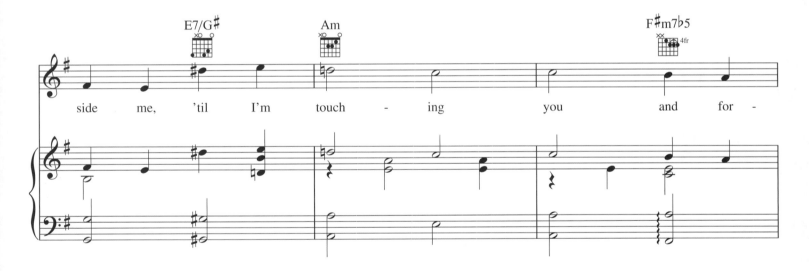

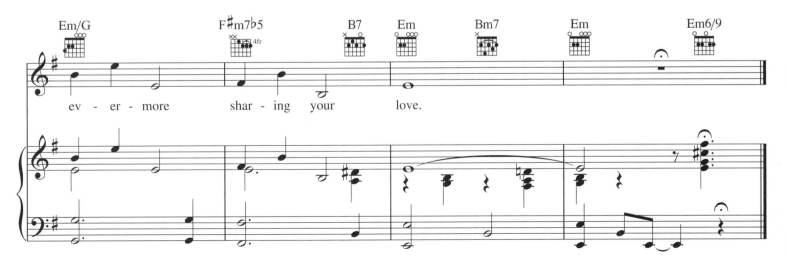

IF WE HOLD ON TOGETHER

from THE LAND BEFORE TIME

Words and Music by JAMES HORNER
and WILL JENNINGS

Flowingly

Don't lose your way with each pass-ing day.
Souls in the wind must learn how to bend,

You've come so far, don't throw it a-way.
seek out a star, hold on to the end.

Live be-liev-ing
Val-ley, moun-tain,

dreams are for weav-ing, won-ders are wait-ing to start.
there is a foun-tain, wash-es our tears all a-way.

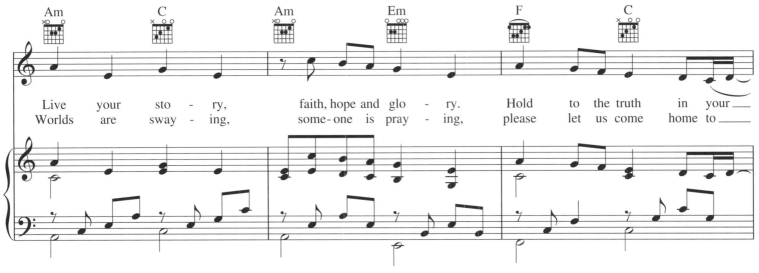

Live your sto - ry, faith, hope and glo - ry. Hold to the truth in your
Worlds are sway - ing, some - one is pray - ing, please let us come home to

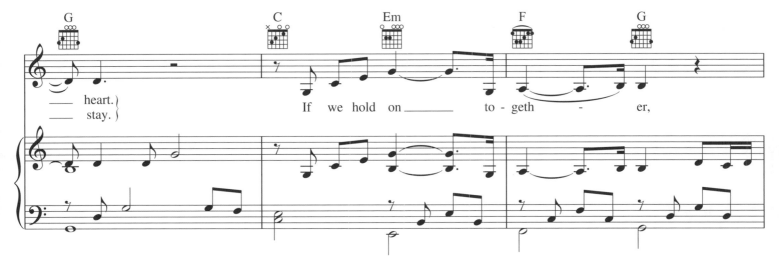

— heart. }
— stay. } If we hold on — to - geth - er,

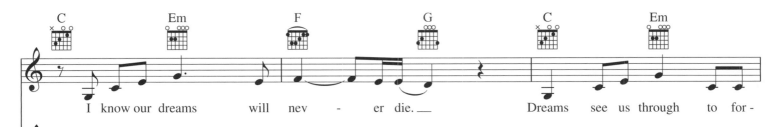

I know our dreams will nev - er die. — Dreams see us through to for -

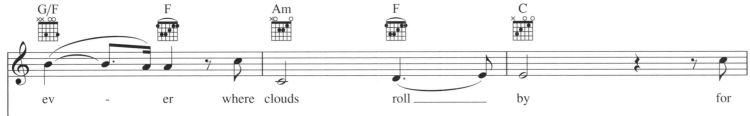

ev - er where clouds roll — by for

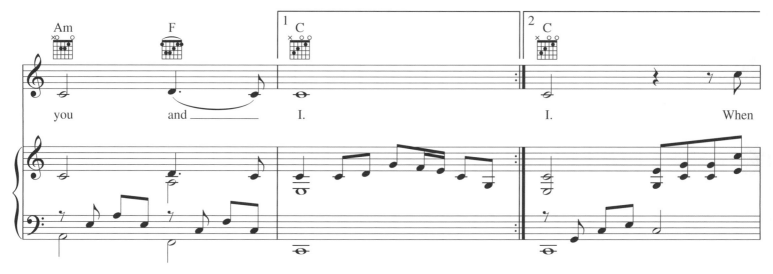

you and _____ I. I. When

we are out there in the dark, __ we'll dream a-bout _____ the sun. __

_____ In the dark we'll feel __ the light, __

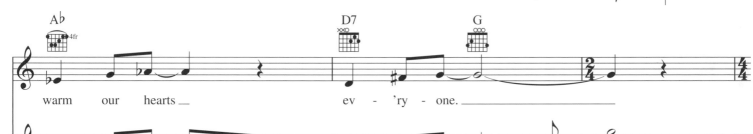

warm our hearts __ ev-'ry-one. _____

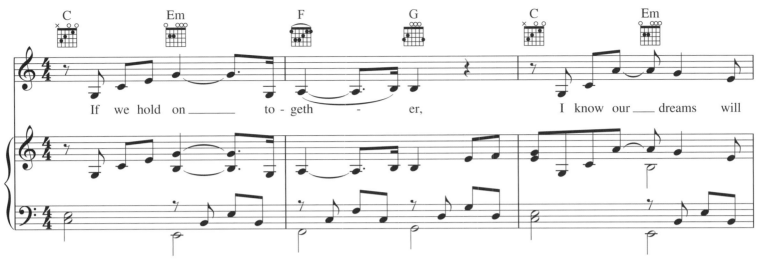

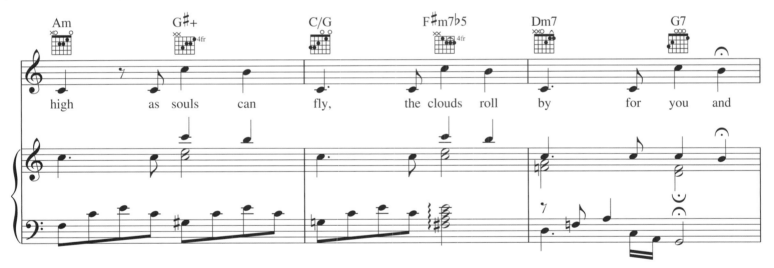

IT MUST HAVE BEEN LOVE

featured in the Motion Picture PRETTY WOMAN

Words and Music by
PER GESSLE

-per on my pil - low, _____ leave the
-ing we're to - geth - er, _____ that I'm shel -

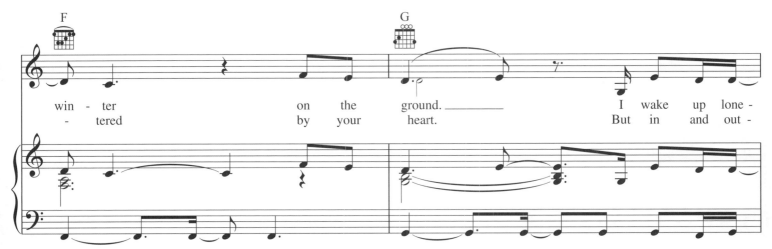

win - ter on the ground. _____ I wake up lone -
-tered by your heart. But in and out -

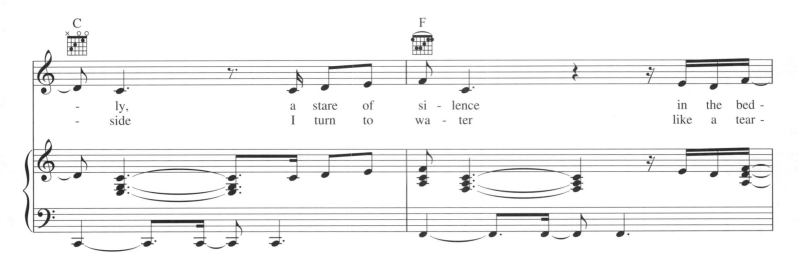

- ly, a stare of si - lence in the bed -
-side I turn to wa - ter like a tear -

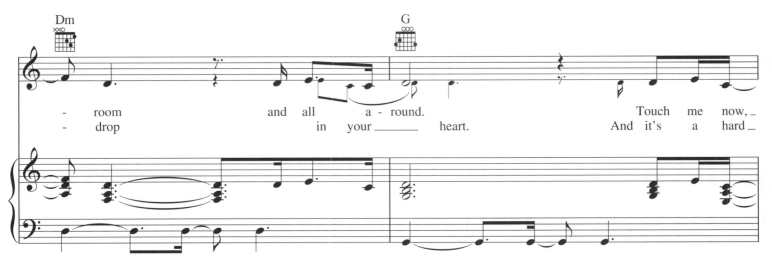

-room and all a - round. Touch me now, _
-drop in your _____ heart. And it's a hard _

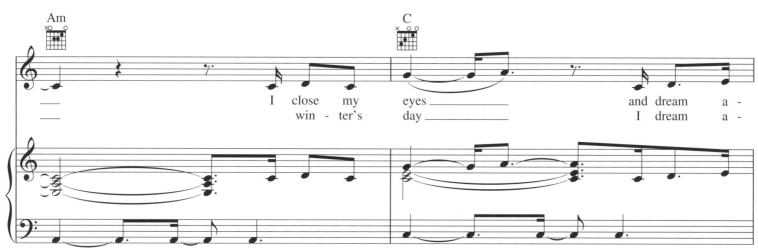

I close my eyes _____ and dream a -
win - ter's day _____ I dream a -

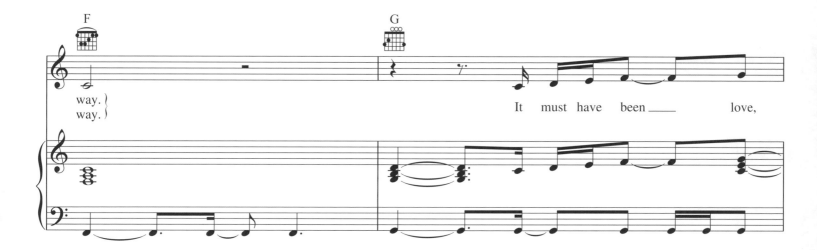

way.
way. It must have been _____ love,

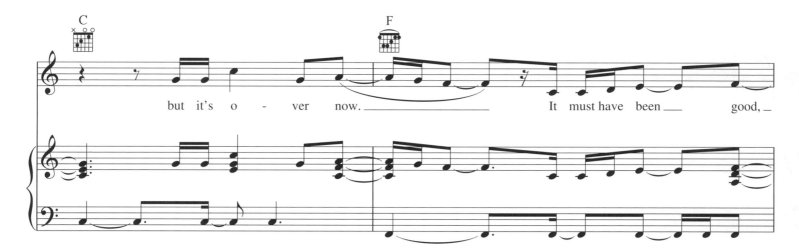

but it's o - ver now. _____ It must have been _____ good, __

__ but I lost it some - how. _____ It must have been _____ love, __

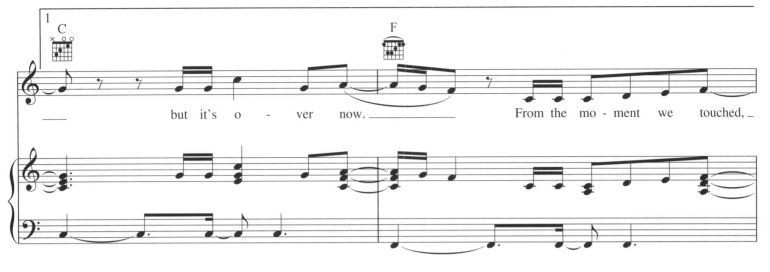

but it's o - ver now. _____ From the mo - ment we touched, _

_ to the time that ran out. _____ Make - be - liev -

_ but it's o - ver now. _____ It's where the wa -

- ter flows. _ It's where the

wind ____ blows. _

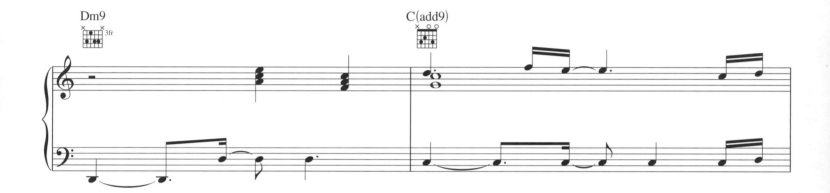

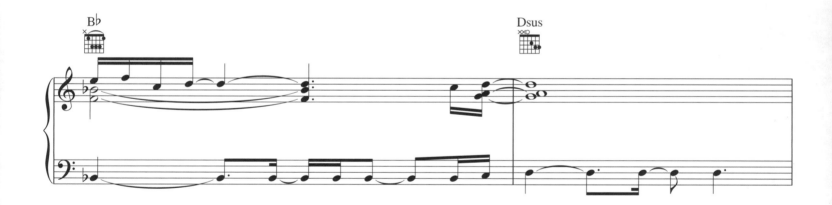

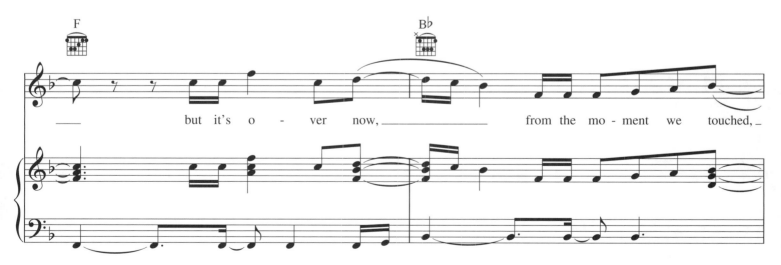

to the time that ran out. _____ Yeah, must have been _____ love, _____

_____ but it's o - ver now. _____ It's all that I want -

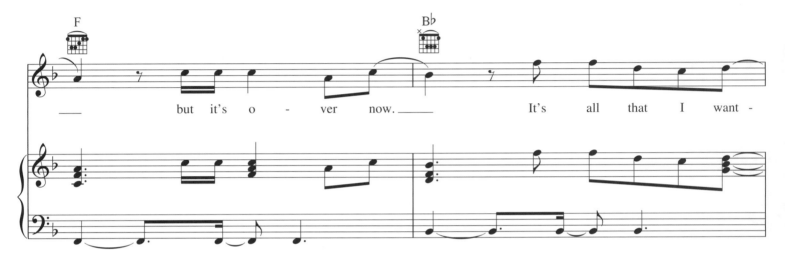

- ed, now I'm liv - ing with - out. _____ It must have been _____ love, _____

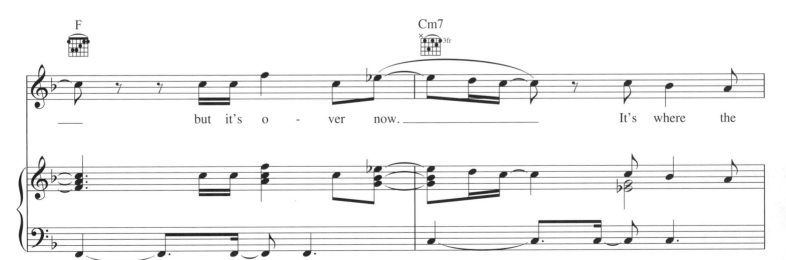

_____ but it's o - ver now. _____ It's where the

wa - ter flows. ___   It's where the   wind ___ blows.

Must have been   love, ___   but it's

o - ver now, ___   now. ___

Optional Ending

Repeat and Fade

THE LAST TIME I FELT LIKE THIS

from SAME TIME, NEXT YEAR

Words by ALAN BERGMAN and MARILYN BERGMAN
Music by MARVIN HAMLISCH

Slow Ballad tempo

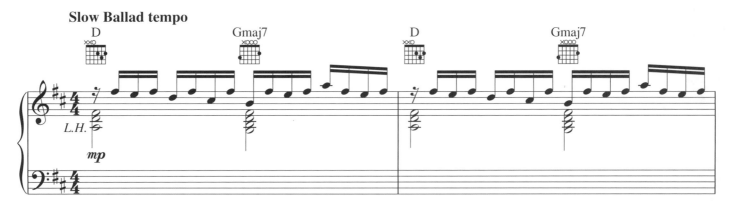

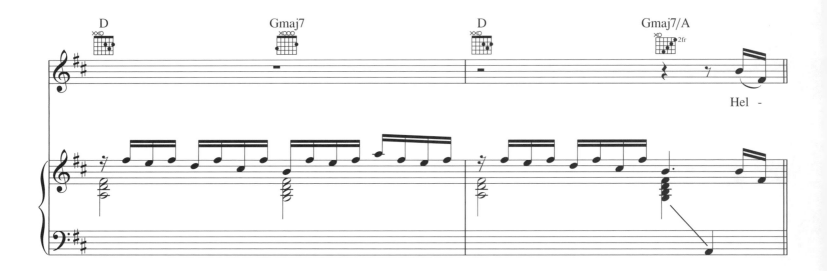

Hel -

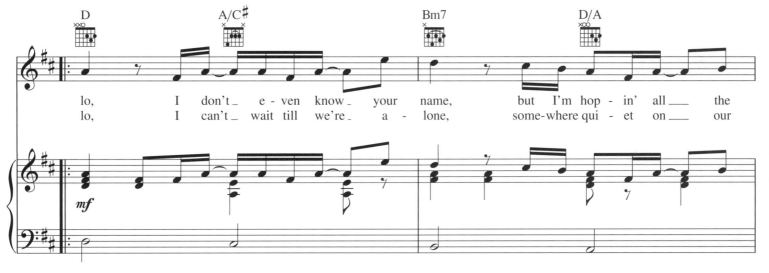

lo, I don't_ e-ven know_ your name, but I'm hop-in' all__ the
lo, I can't_ wait till we're_ a - lone, some-where qui-et on__ our

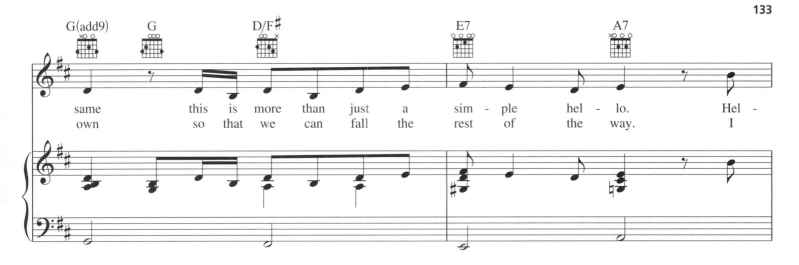

same   this is more than just a sim- ple hel- lo.   Hel-
own   so that we can fall the rest of the way.   I

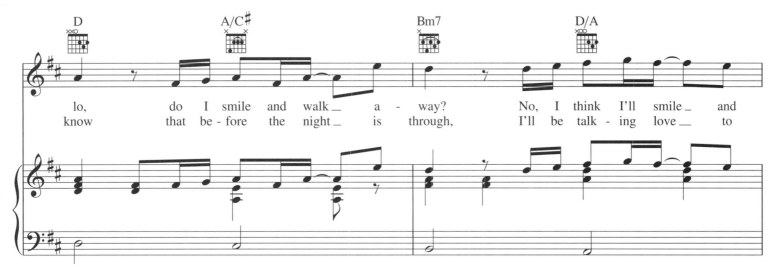

lo,   do I smile and walk __ a-way?   No, I think I'll smile __ and
know   that be-fore the night __ is through,   I'll be talk-ing love __ to

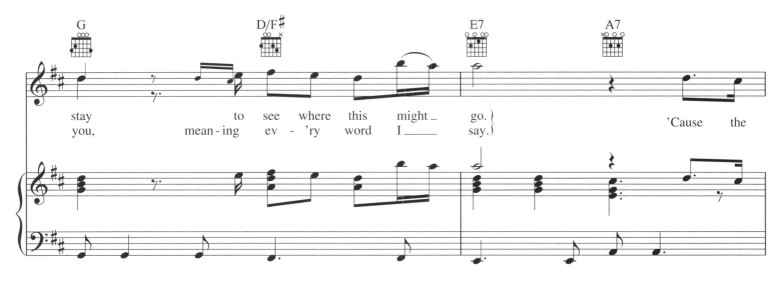

stay   to see where this might __ go.)
you,   mean-ing ev-'ry word I ____ say.)   'Cause the

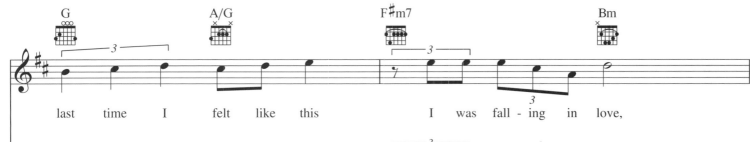

last time I felt like this   I was fall-ing in love,

falling and feel - ing ____ I'd nev - er fall in love a - gain. Yes, the

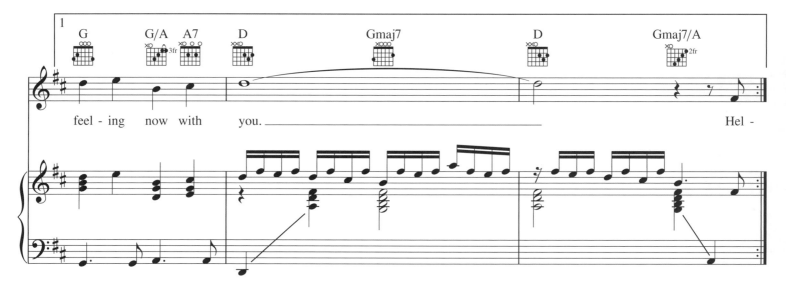

last time I felt like this was long be - fore I knew ___ what I'm

feel - ing now with you. _____ Hel -

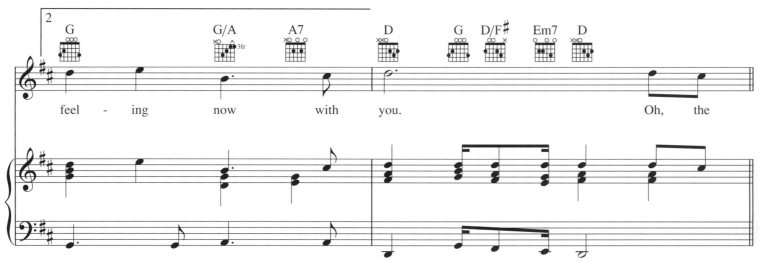

feel - ing now with you. Oh, the

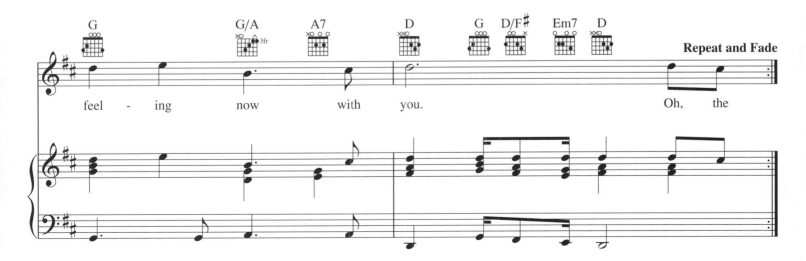

THE LOOK OF LOVE

from CASINO ROYALE

Words by HAL DAVID
Music by BURT BACHARACH

Medium Rock Ballad, with much feeling

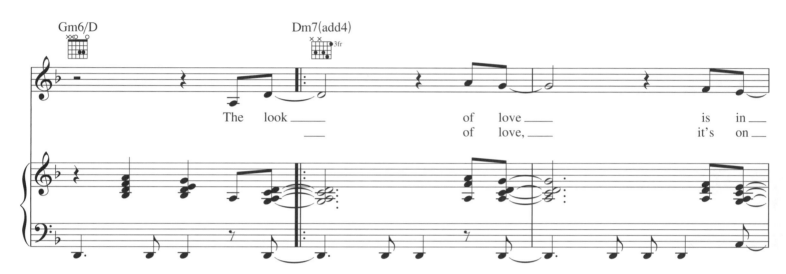

The look _____ of love _____ is in _____
_____ of love, _____ it's on _____

_____ your eyes, _____ a look _____ your smile _____
_____ your face, _____ a look _____ that time _____

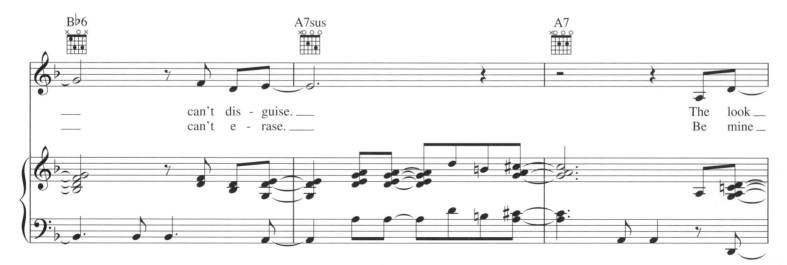

_____ can't dis - guise. _____ The look
_____ can't e - rase. _____ Be mine

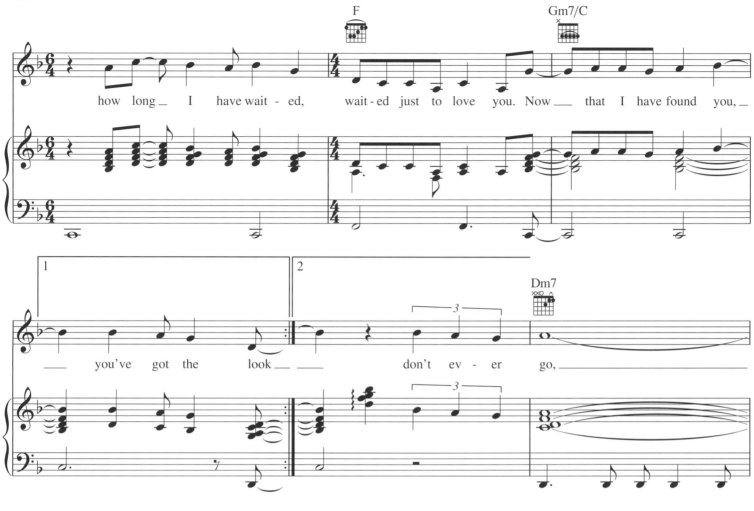

how long __ I have wait - ed, wait - ed just to love you. Now __ that I have found you, __

1.
__ you've got the look __
2.
__ don't ev - er go, __

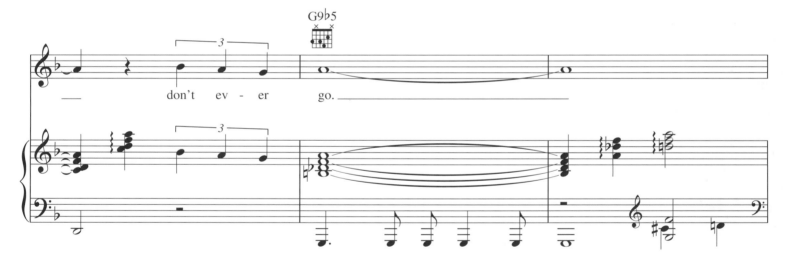

__ don't ev - er go. __

I love you so. __

NOT GON' CRY

from the Original Soundtrack Album WAITING TO EXHALE

Words and Music by
BABYFACE

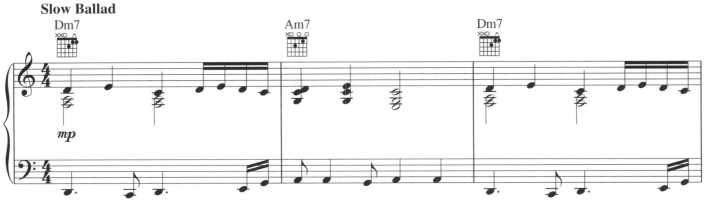

(1.) While all the time that I was lov - ing you, ___
(2., D.S.) I was your lov - er and your sec - re - tar - y,

you were bus - y lov - ing your - self. ___
work - ing ev - 'ry day of the week. ___

I would stop breath - ing if you told ___ me to, ___
Was at the job when no one else ___ was there, ___

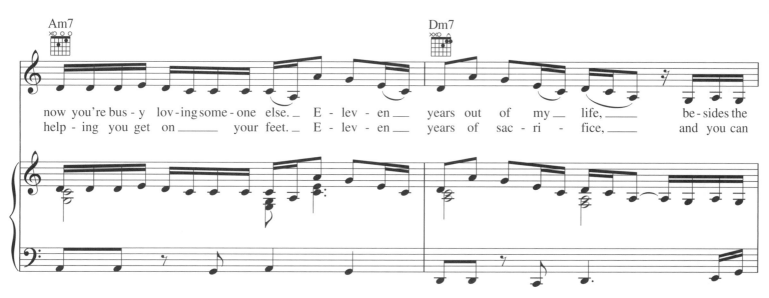

now you're bus - y lov-ing some - one else. __ E - lev - en __ years out of my __ life, ____ be - sides the
help - ing you get on _____ your feet. __ E - lev - en __ years of sac - ri - fice, ____ and you can

kids, I have noth - ing to show. Wast - ed my __ years, a fool of a wife. ____ I should - a
leave me at the drop of a dime. Swal - lowed my __ fears, stood by your __ side. ____ I should - a

To Coda ⊕

left your ass long time a - go. ____ } Well, I'm not gon' cry, I'm not gon' cry. I'm
left your ass a thou - sand times. ____ }

not gon' shed no tears. No, I'm not gon' cry, it's not the time ___ 'cause

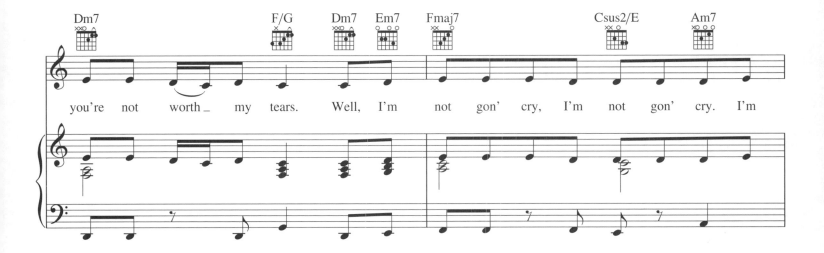

you're not worth ___ my tears. Well, I'm not gon' cry, I'm not gon' cry. I'm

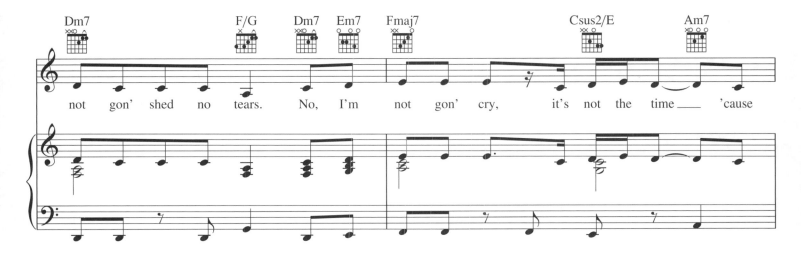

not gon' shed no tears. No, I'm not gon' cry, it's not the time ___ 'cause

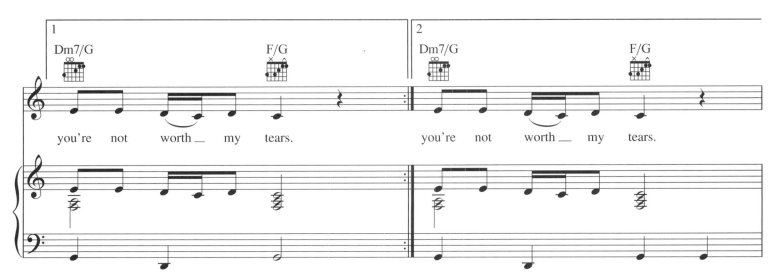

1.

you're not worth ___ my tears.

2.

you're not worth ___ my tears.

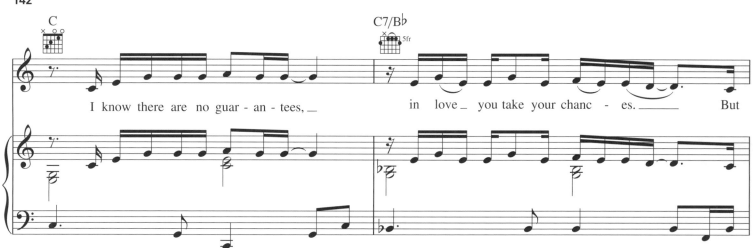

I know there are no guar - an - tees, ___ in love ___ you take your chanc - es. _____ But

some-how it seems un-fair ___ to me, so ___ un-fair, look at the cir-cum-stanc - es. _____ Through

sick-ness and health, 'til death do us part, those were the words that we said from our heart. So

now when you say ___ that you're leav-ing me, ___ I don't ___ get that part, ___ oh. _____

D.S. al Coda
(take 2nd verse)

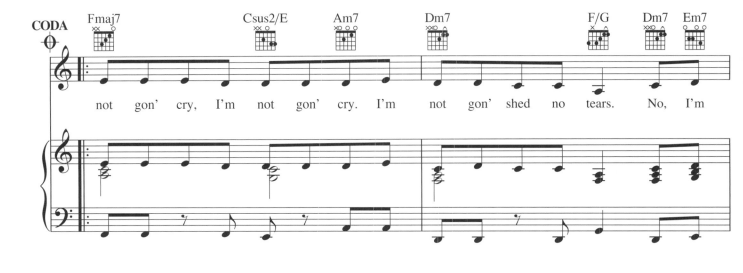

LOVE ME TENDER

from LOVE ME TENDER

Words and Music by ELVIS PRESLEY
and VERA MATSON

Moderately slow

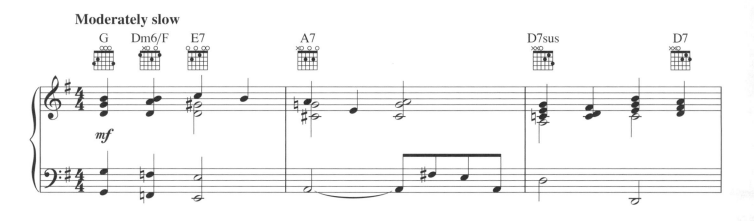

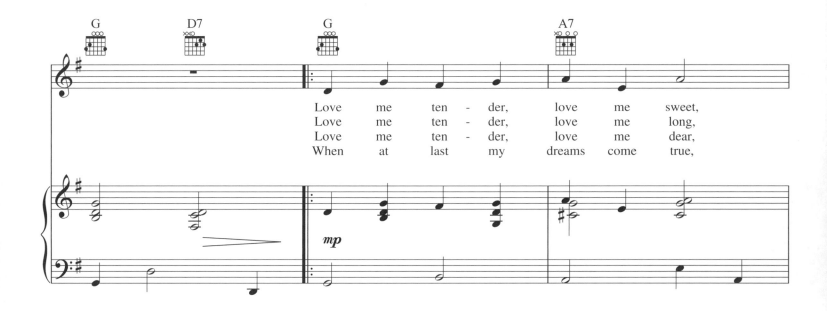

Love me ten - der, love me sweet,
Love me ten - der, love me long,
Love me ten - der, love me dear,
When at last my dreams come true,

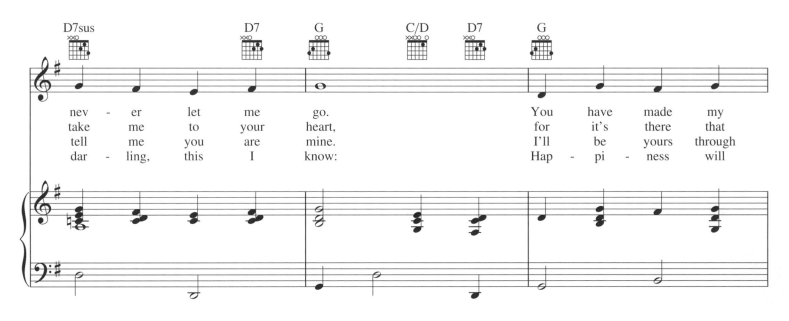

nev - er let me go.
take me to your heart,
tell me you are mine.
dar - ling, this I know:

You have made my
for it's made there that
I'll be yours through
Hap - pi - ness will

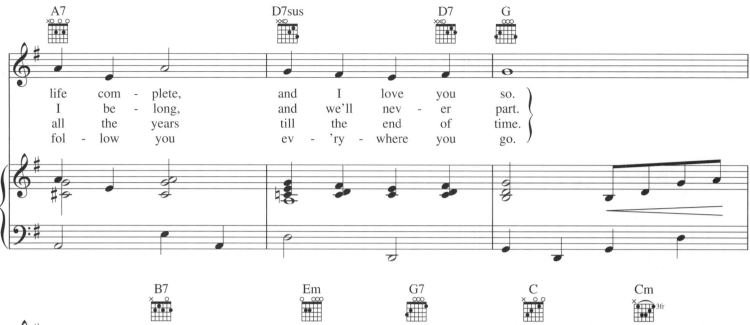

life com - plete, and I love you so.
I be - long, and we'll nev - er so part.
all the years till the end of time.
fol - low you ev - 'ry - where you go.

Love me ten - der, love me true, all my dreams ful -

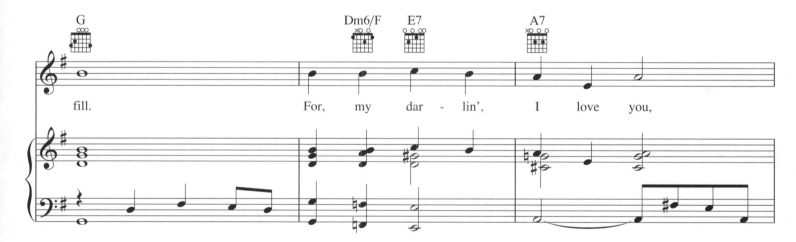

fill. For, my dar - lin', I love you,

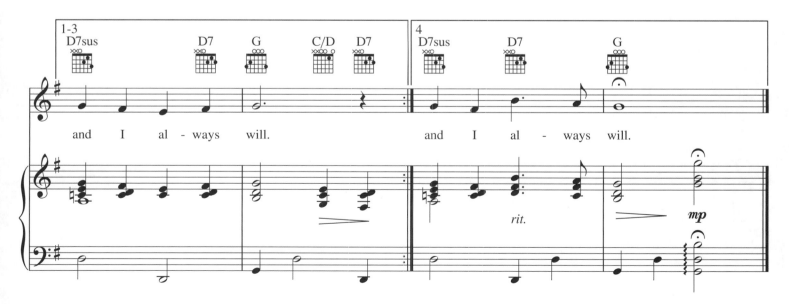

and I al - ways will.

and I al - ways will.

A MAN AND A WOMAN

(Un homme et une femme)

from A MAN AND A WOMAN

Original Words by PIERRE BAROUH
English Words by JERRY KELLER
Music by FRANCIS LAI

When hearts are pass-ing in the night, in the lone-ly night,_____ then they must
si-lence of the mist, of the morn-ing mist,_____ when lips are

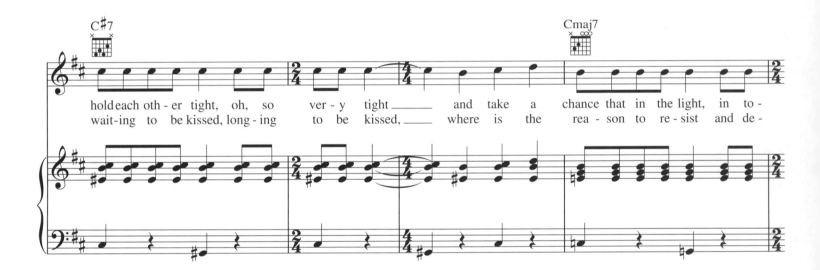

hold each oth-er tight, oh, so ver-y tight_____ and take a chance that in the light, in to-
wait-ing to be kissed, long-ing to be kissed,_____ where is the rea-son to re-sist and de-

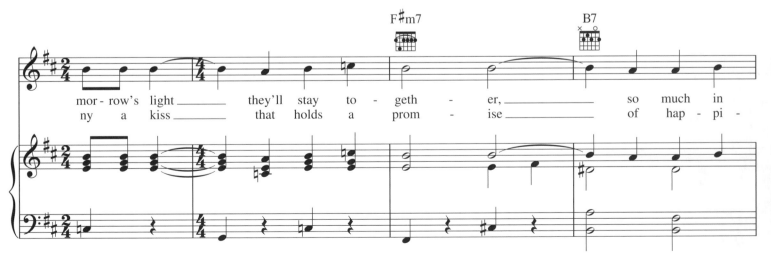

mor-row's light_____ they'll stay to-geth-er,_____ so much in
ny a kiss_____ that holds a prom-ise_____ of hap-pi-

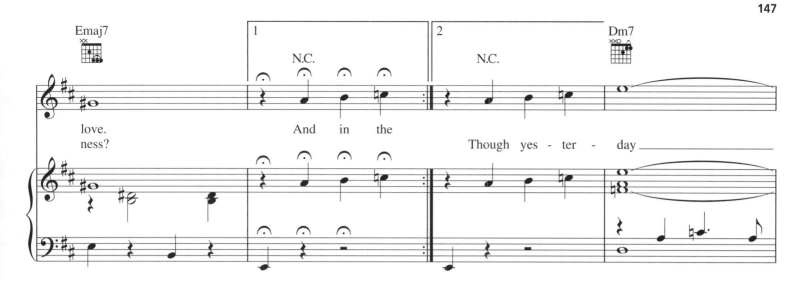

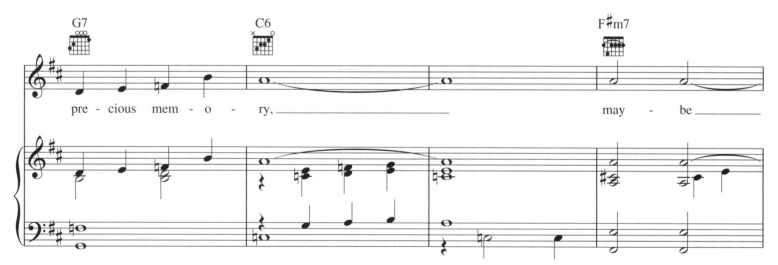

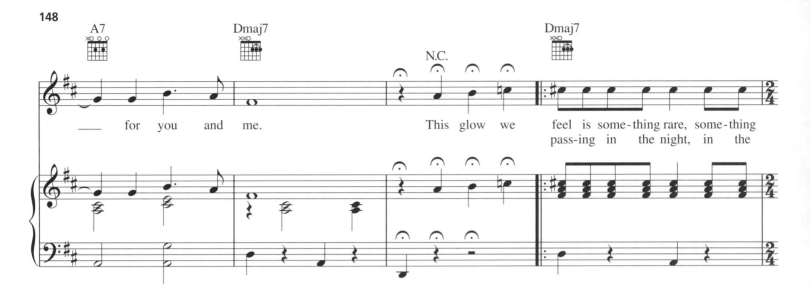

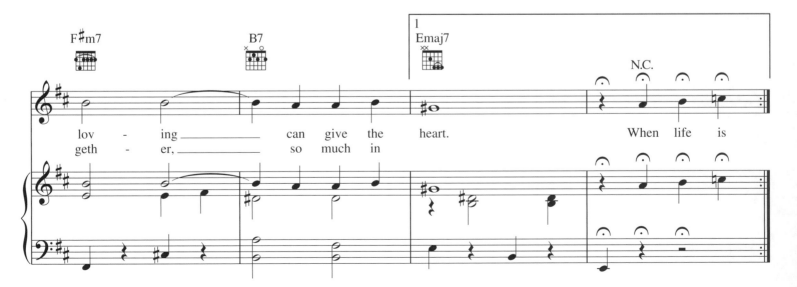

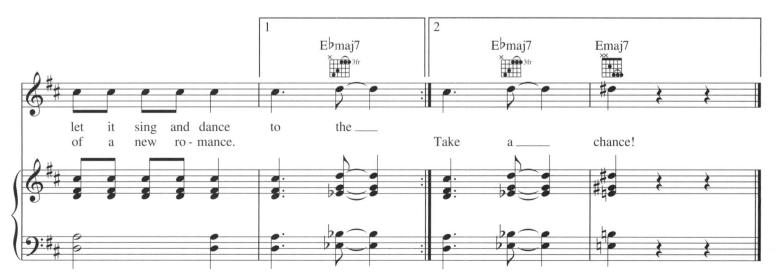

THE MUSIC OF GOODBYE
Love Theme from OUT OF AFRICA

Music by JOHN BARRY
Words by ALAN and MARILYN BERGMAN

Medium slow Ballad

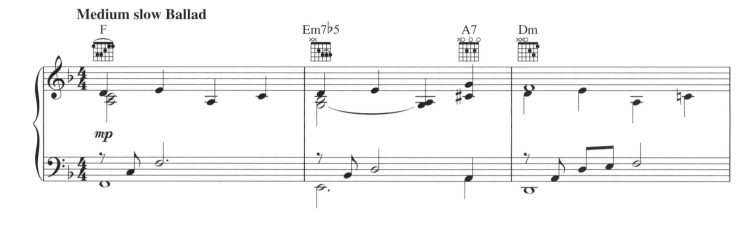

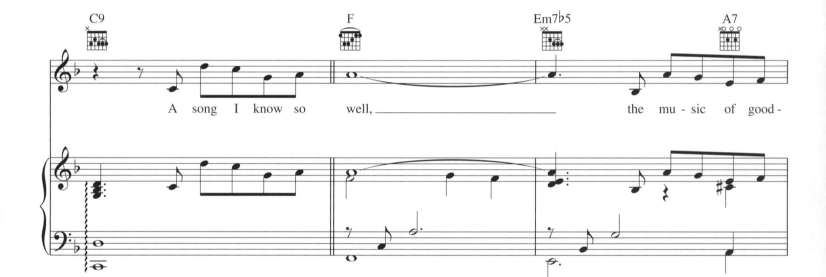

A song I know so well, _____ the mu-sic of good-

bye a - gain. _____ It's there each time we say "Hel - lo." _____

As al-ways there's no rea-son why a-gain.

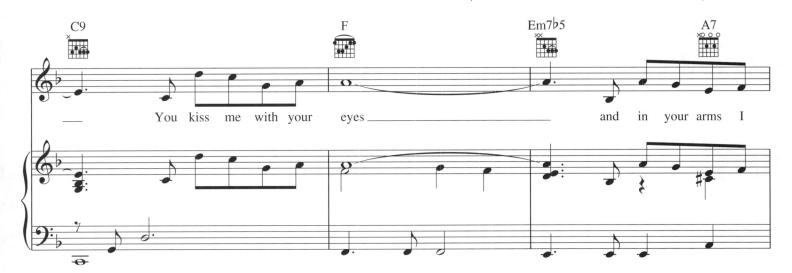

You kiss me with your eyes and in your arms I

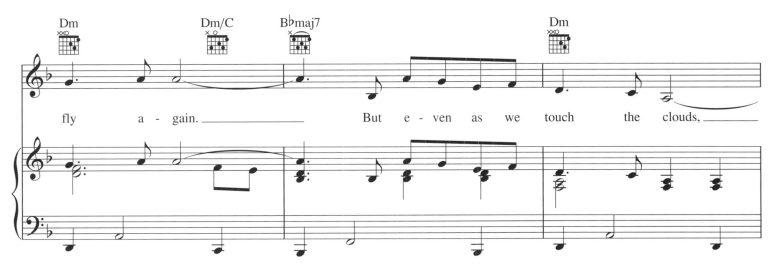

fly a-gain. But e-ven as we touch the clouds,

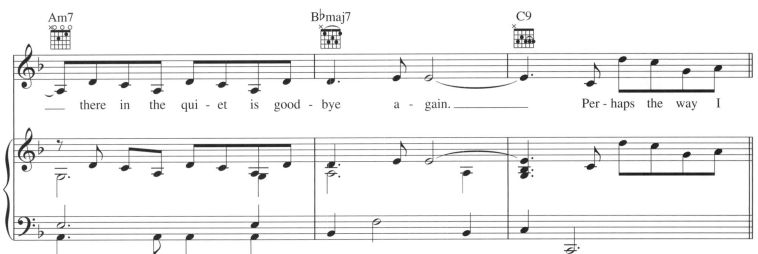

there in the qui-et is good-bye a-gain. Per-haps the way I

hold you _____ makes you a-fraid I'll hold you; _____

_____ makes you a-fraid to love me. _____

Love me. _____ As through the night we dance, _____

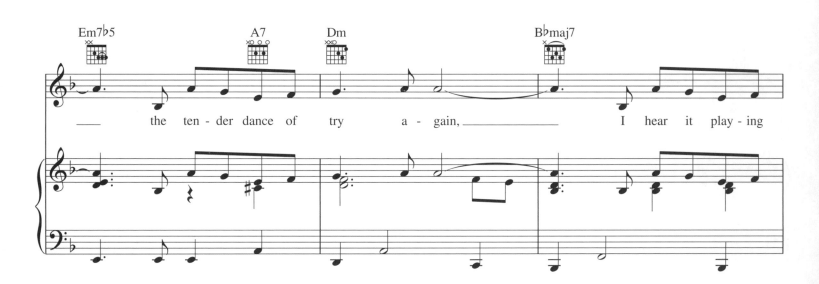

_____ the ten-der dance of try a-gain, _____ I hear it play-ing

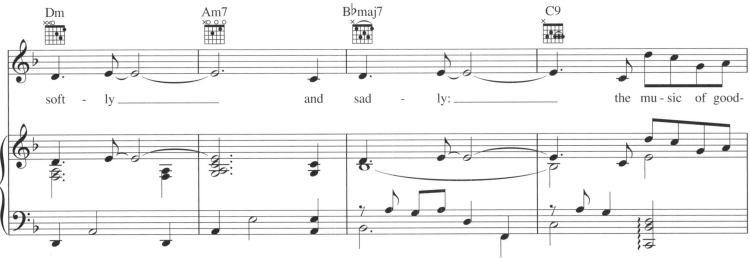

soft - ly _____ and sad - ly: _____ the mu - sic of good-

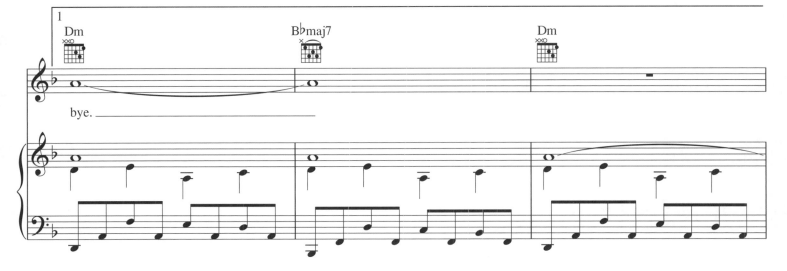

bye. _____

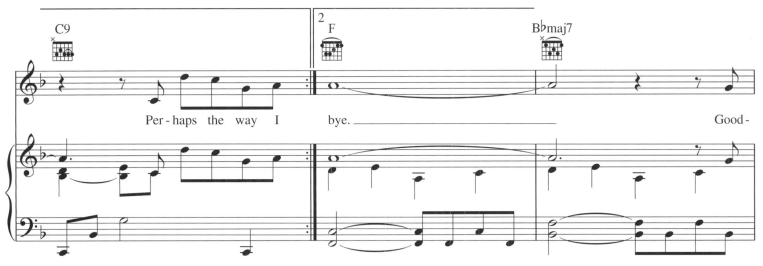

Per - haps the way I bye. _____ Good-

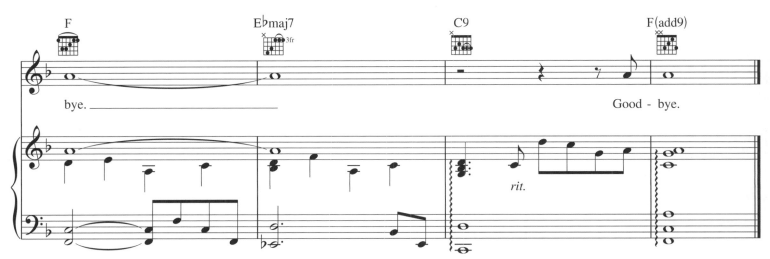

bye. _____ Good - bye.

rit.

MY HEART WILL GO ON
(Love Theme from 'Titanic')
from the Paramount and Twentieth Century Fox Motion Picture TITANIC

Music by JAMES HORNER
Lyric by WILL JENNINGS

Moderately

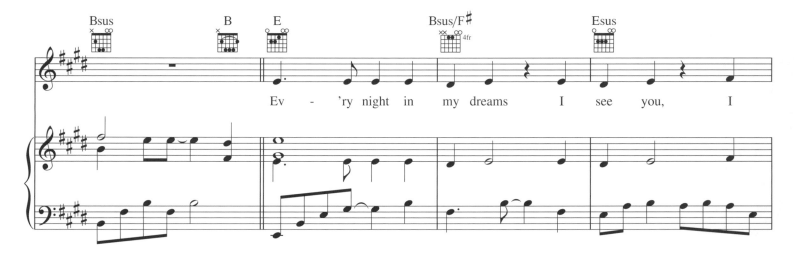

Ev - 'ry night in my dreams I see you, I

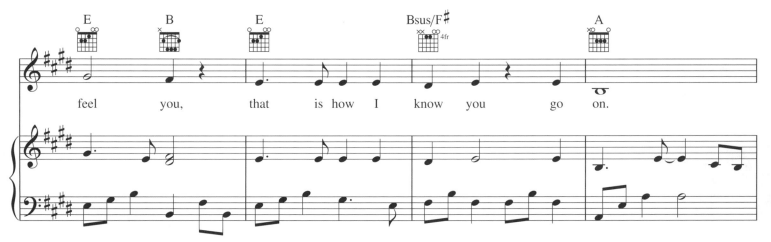

feel you, that is how I know you go on.

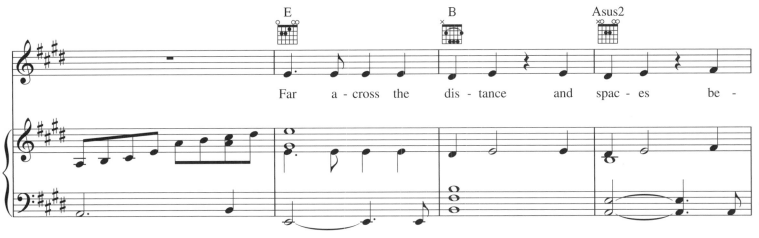

Far a-cross the dis-tance and spac-es be-

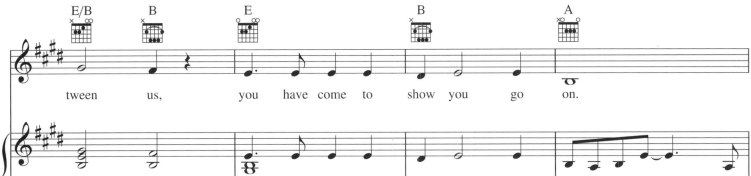

tween us, you have come to show you go on.

Near, far, wher-ev-er you are,

I be-lieve that the heart does go on.

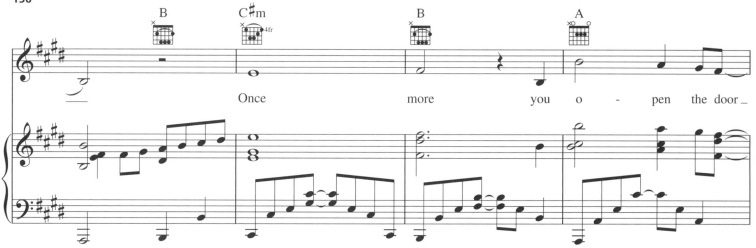

Once more you o - pen the door __

__ and you're here in my heart, and my heart will go

on and on.

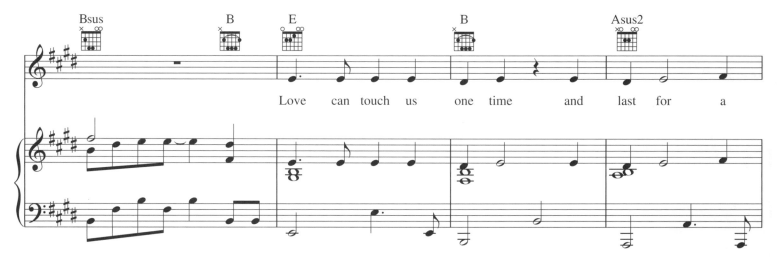

Love can touch us one time and last for a

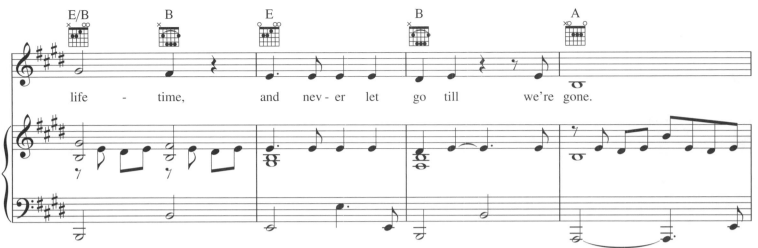

life - time, and nev - er let go till we're gone.

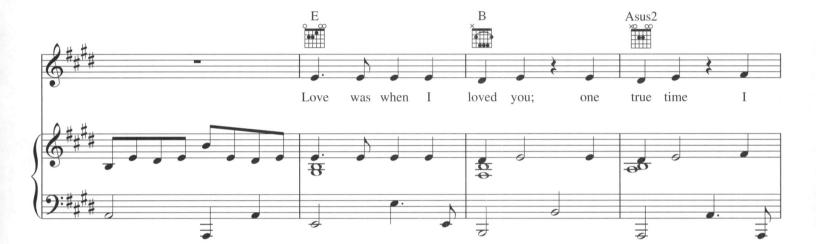

Love was when I loved you; one true time I

hold to. In my life we'll al - ways go on.

D.S. al Coda

CODA

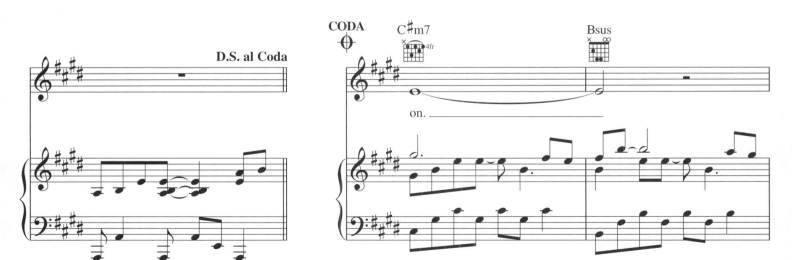

on.

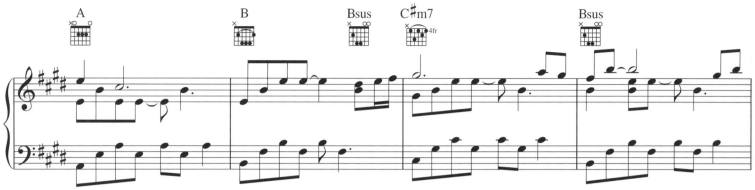

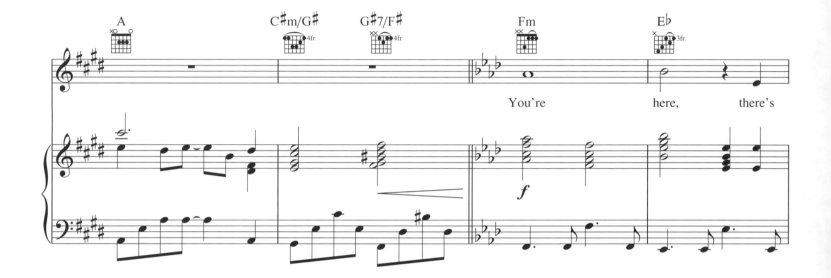

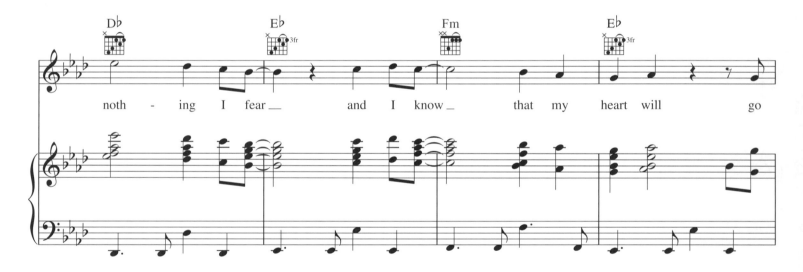

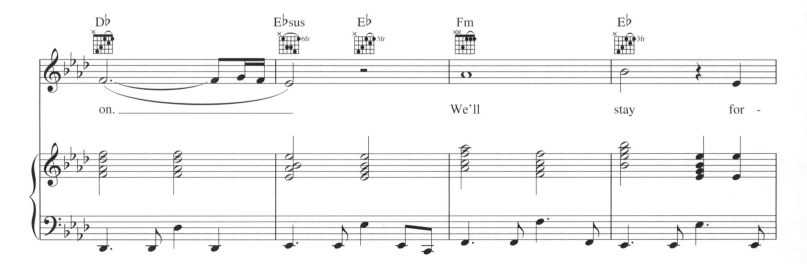

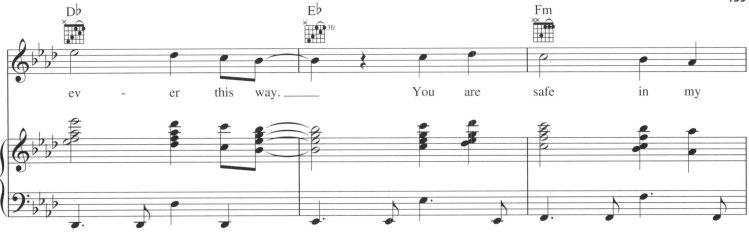

ev - er this way. _____ You are safe in my

heart, and my heart will go on and on. _____

ff decrescendo to end

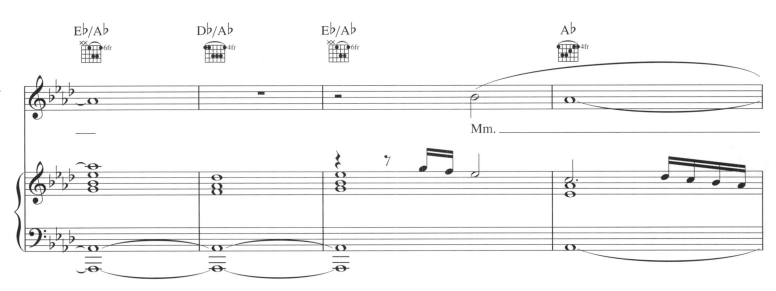

Mm.

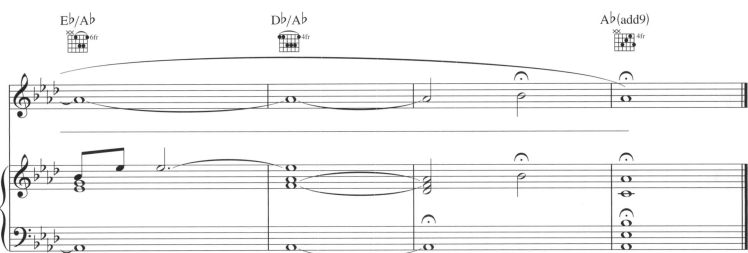

THE PROMISE
(I'll Never Say Goodbye)
Theme from the Universal Picture THE PROMISE

Words by ALAN and MARILYN BERGMAN
Music by DAVID SHIRE

*Cue notes optional 2nd time

READY TO TAKE A CHANCE AGAIN
(Love Theme)
from the Paramount Picture FOUL PLAY

Words by NORMAN GIMBEL
Music by CHARLES FOX

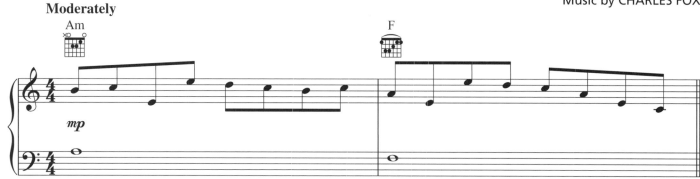

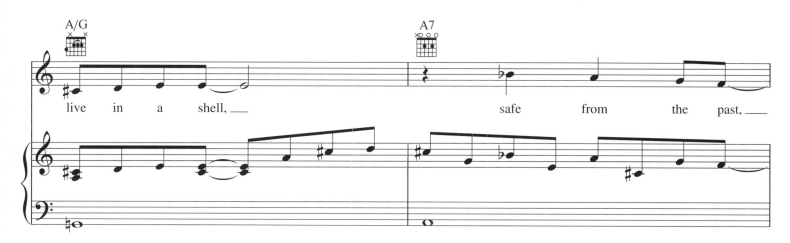

You re-mind ___ me ___ I

live in a shell, ___ safe from the past, ___

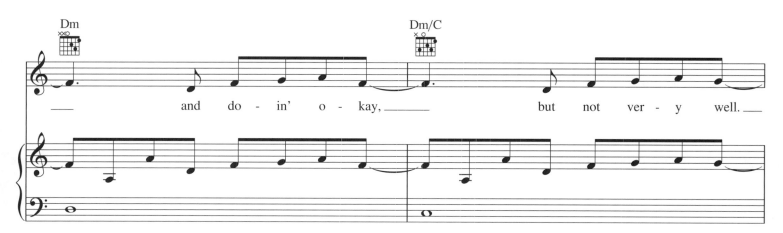

___ and do-in' o-kay, ___ but not ver-y well. ___

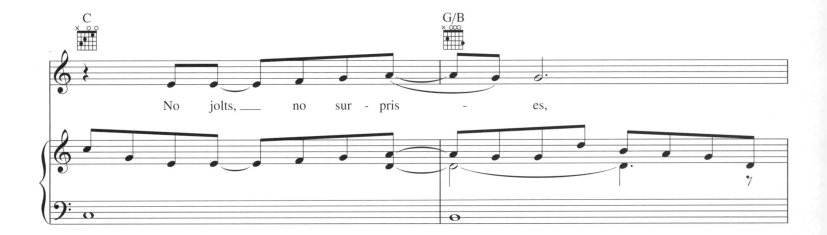

No jolts, ___ no sur - pris - es,

no cri - sis a - ris - es. My life ___ goes a - long ___

___ as it should, __ it's all ver - y nice, ___ but

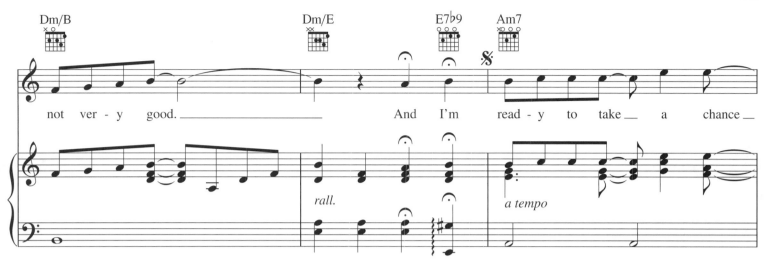

not ver - y good. _____ And I'm read - y to take __ a chance __

__ a - gain, __ read - y to put __ my love ____ on the line ___ with

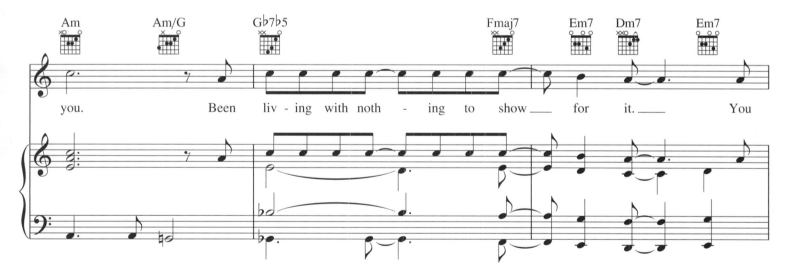

you. Been liv - ing with noth - ing to show ___ for it. ___ You

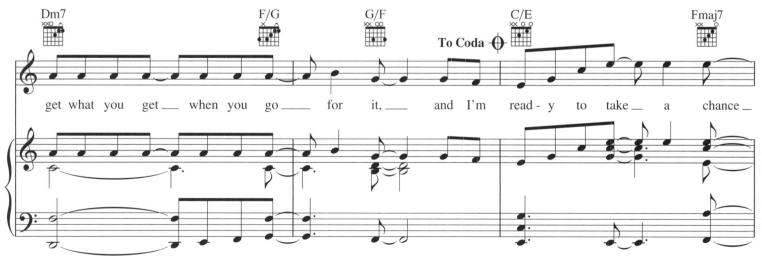

get what you get __ when you go __ for it, ___ and I'm read - y to take __ a chance __

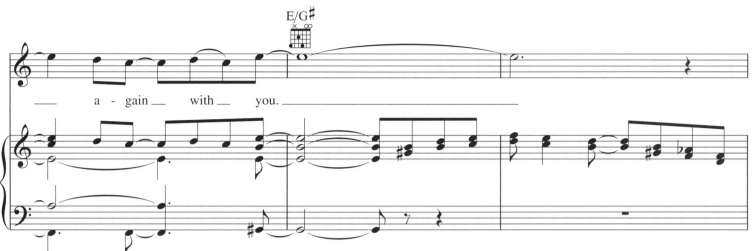

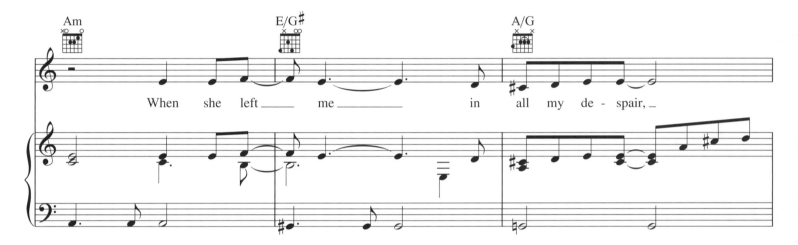

a - gain __ with __ you. ____

When she left ____ me ____ in all my de - spair, __

A7   Dm   Dm/C

I just held on. My hopes were all gone, ____ then

D.S. al Coda

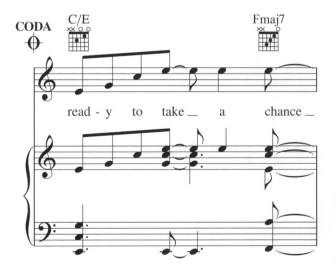

I found you there. ____ And I'm

read - y to take __ a chance __

167

a - gain, ready to take a chance a - gain with you,

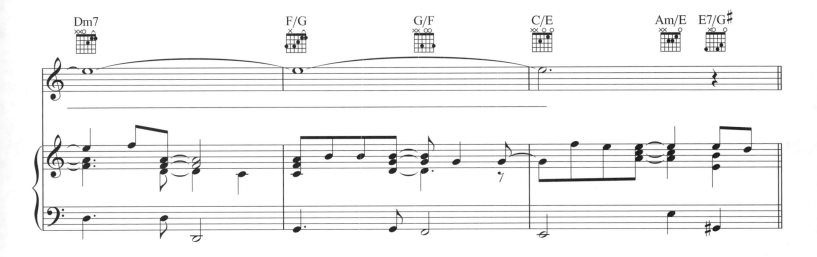

with you.

Repeat ad lib. and Fade

SAY YOU, SAY ME
from the Motion Picture WHITE NIGHTS

Words and Music by
LIONEL RICHIE

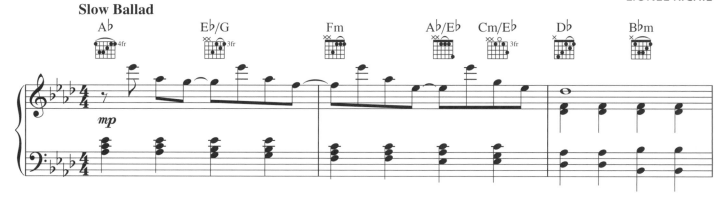

Slow Ballad

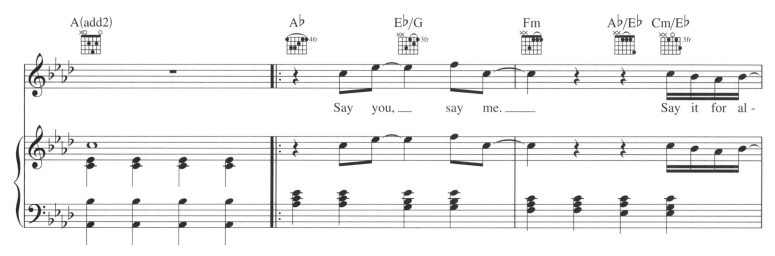

Say you, ___ say me. ___ Say it for al-

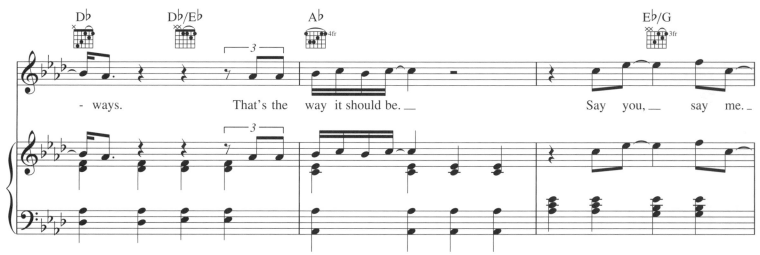

-ways. That's the way it should be. ___ Say you, ___ say me. ___

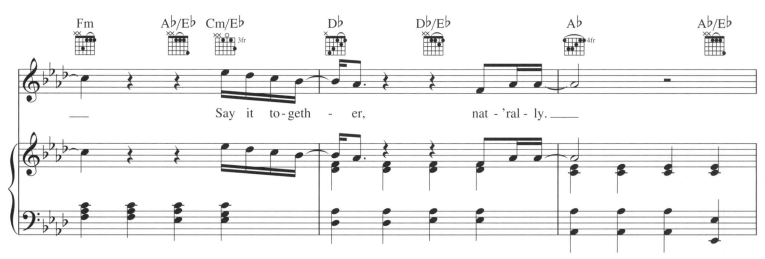

___ Say it to-geth- er, nat-'ral-ly. ___

I had a dream, I had an awe-some dream:
As we go down life's lone-some high-way, seems the

peo-ple in the park play-in' games in the dark.
hard-est thing to do is to find a friend or two,

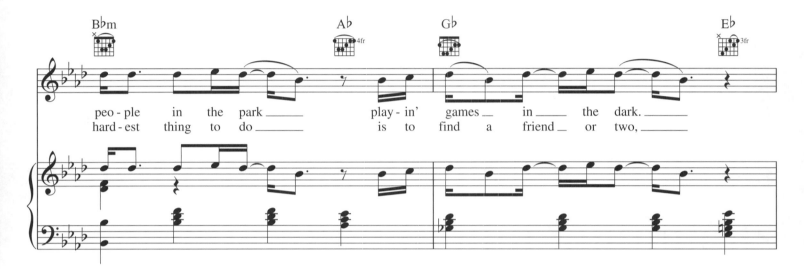

And what they played was a mas-quer-ade.
that help-ing hand, some-one who un-der-stands. But from be-
And when you

hind the walls of doubt, a voice was cry-ing out.
feel you've lost your way, you've got

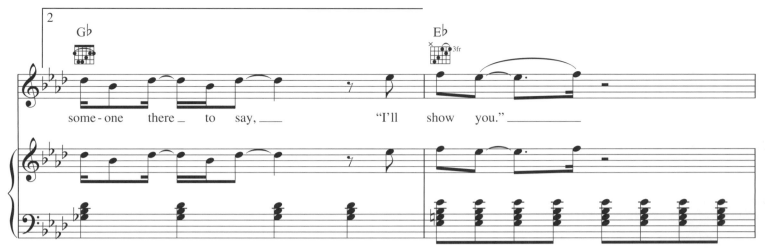

some-one there _ to say, _ "I'll show you." ____

Say you, ____ say me. ____ Say it for al -

- ways. That's the way it should be. ____

Say you, ____ say me. ____ Say it to-geth-

To Coda

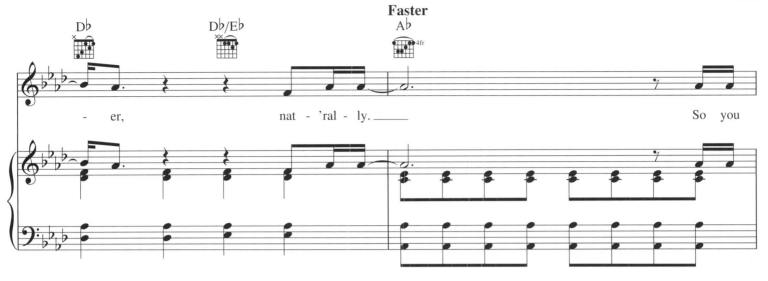

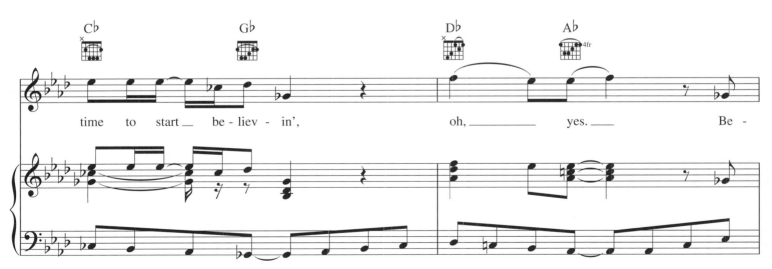

Tempo I

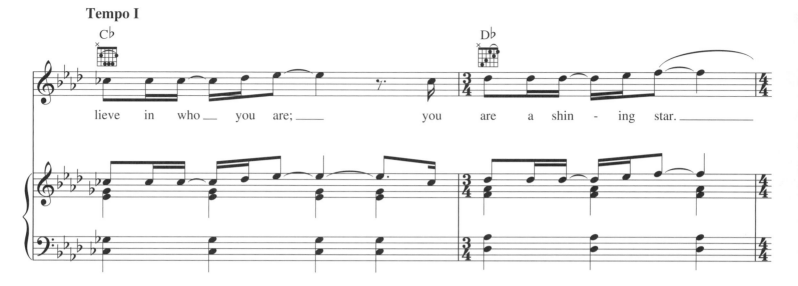

lieve in who __ you are; ___ you are a shin - ing star. _____

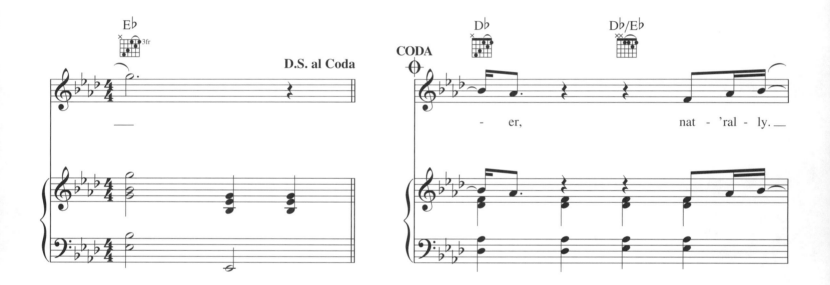

D.S. al Coda

CODA

- er, nat - 'ral - ly. __

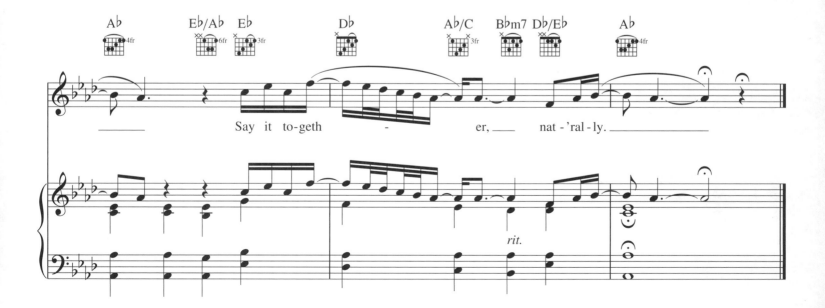

Say it to-geth - er, ___ nat -'ral - ly. _____

rit.

SOMEWHERE OUT THERE
from AN AMERICAN TAIL

Music by BARRY MANN and JAMES HORNER
Lyrics by CYNTHIA WEIL

Moderately, with expression

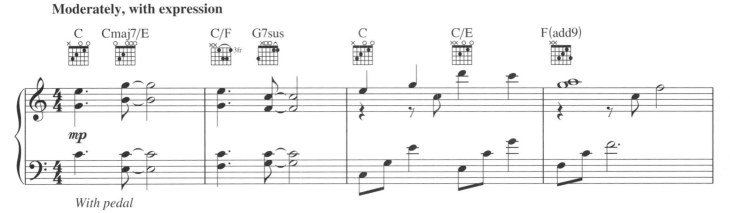

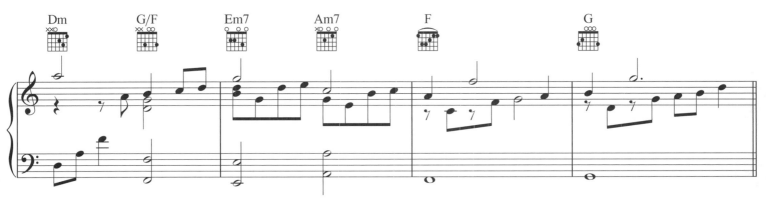

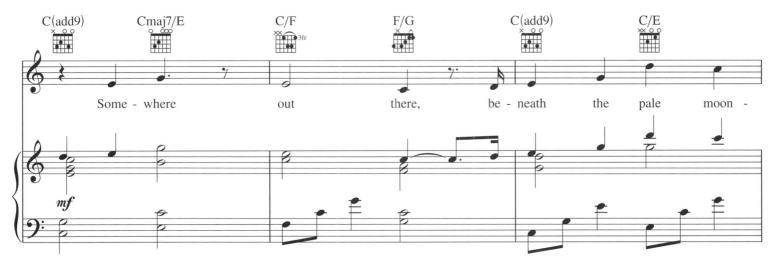

Some - where   out   there,   be - neath the   pale   moon -

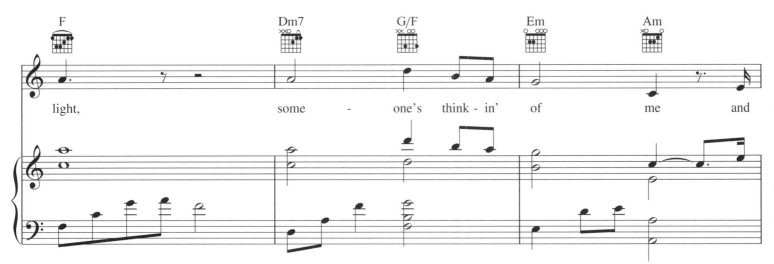

light,   some - one's think - in' of   me   and

lov - ing me to - night. Some - where out

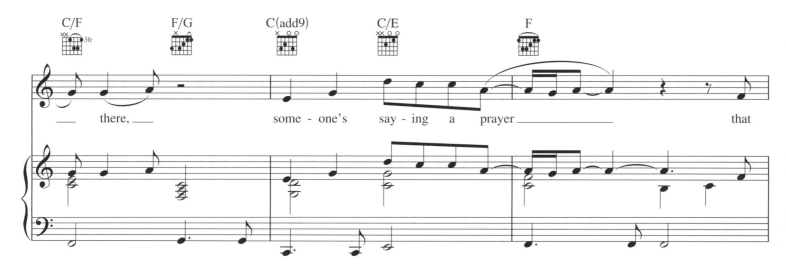

there, some - one's say - ing a prayer that

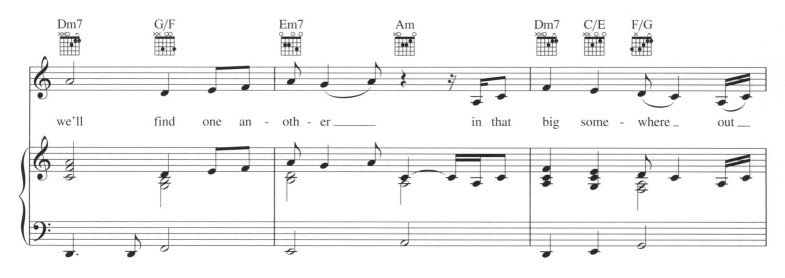

we'll find one an - oth - er in that big some - where out

there. And e - ven though I know how ver - y far a - part we are it

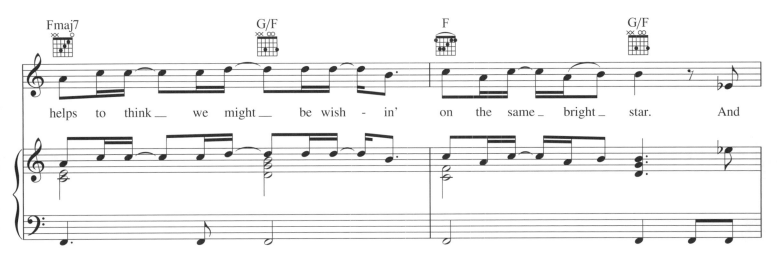

helps to think ___ we might ___ be wish - in' on the same ___ bright ___ star. And

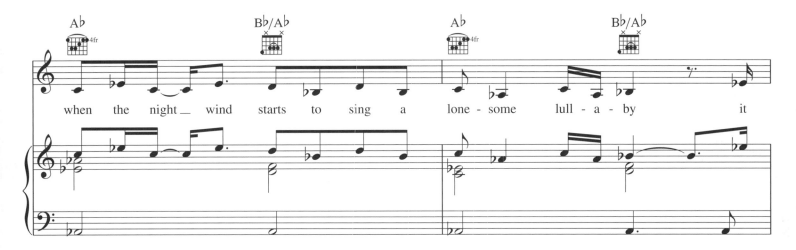

when the night ___ wind starts to sing a lone - some lull - a - by it

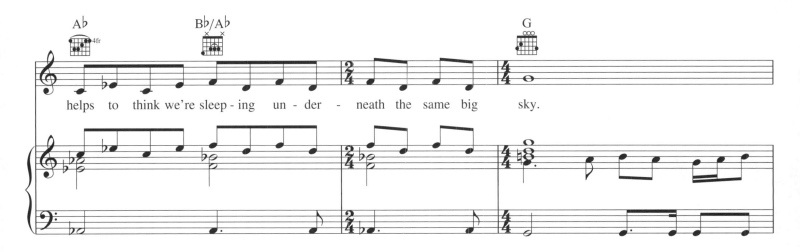

helps to think we're sleep - ing un - der - neath the same big sky.

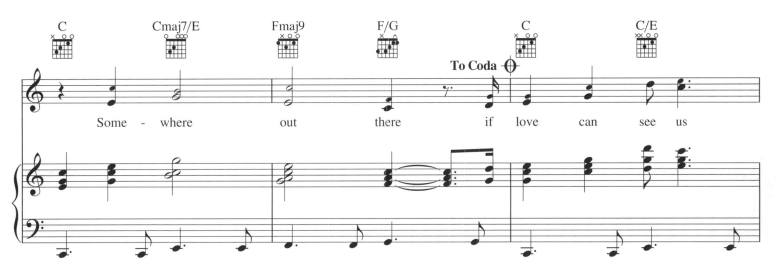

Some - where out there if love can see us

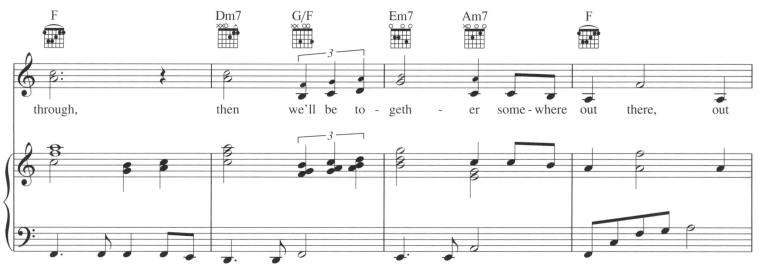

through, then we'll be to-geth - er some-where out there, out

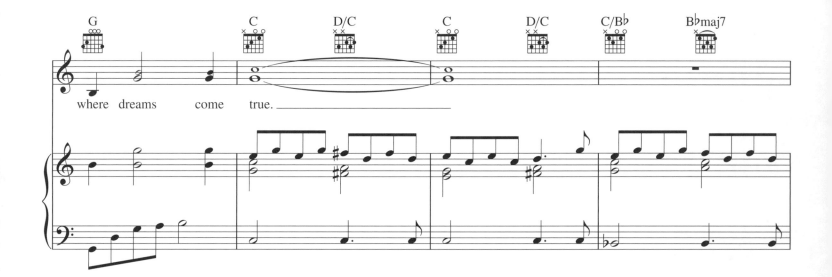

where dreams come true.

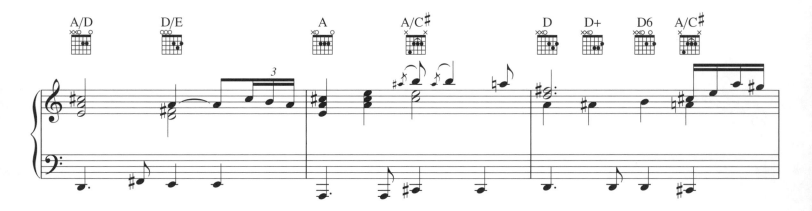

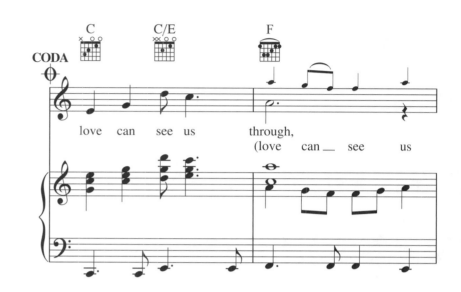

And

love can see us through, (love can __ see us

then we'll be to-geth — er some-where out there, out where dreams come
through)

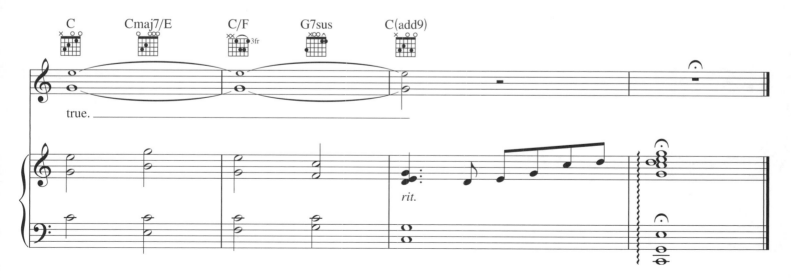

true. _____

SEEMS LIKE OLD TIMES

from ANNIE HALL
from ARTHUR GODFREY AND HIS FRIENDS

Words and Music by JOHN JACOB LOEB
and CARMEN LOMBARDO

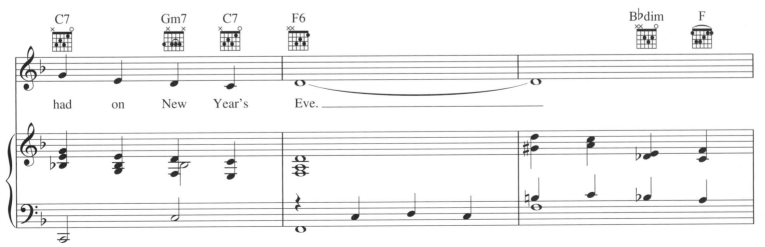

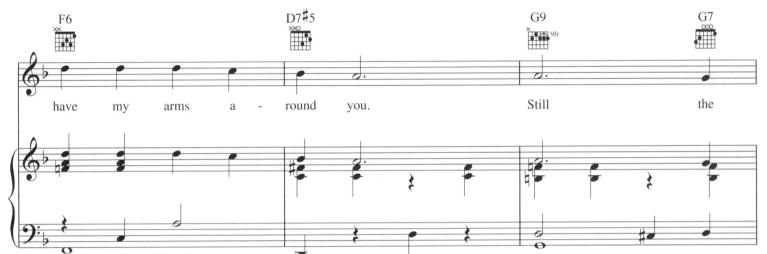

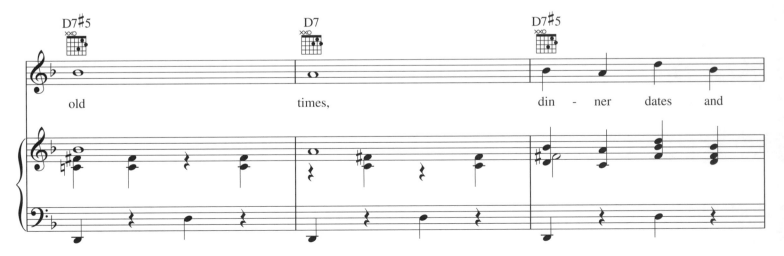

SPEAK SOFTLY, LOVE
(Love Theme)
from the Paramount Picture THE GODFATHER

Words by LARRY KUSIK
Music by NINO ROTA

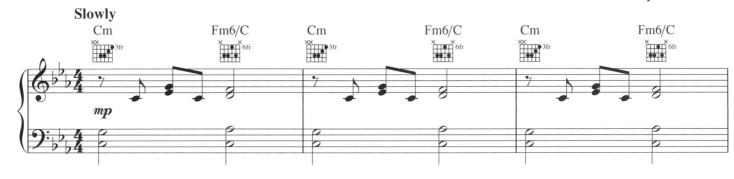

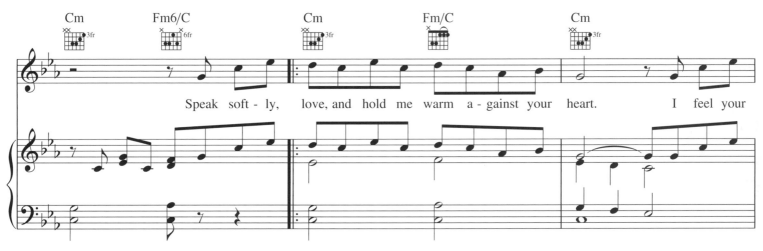

Speak soft-ly, love, and hold me warm a-gainst your heart. I feel your

words, the ten-der, trem-bling mo-ments start. We're in a world _____ our ver-y

own, shar-ing a love that on-ly few have ev-er known. Wine-col-ored

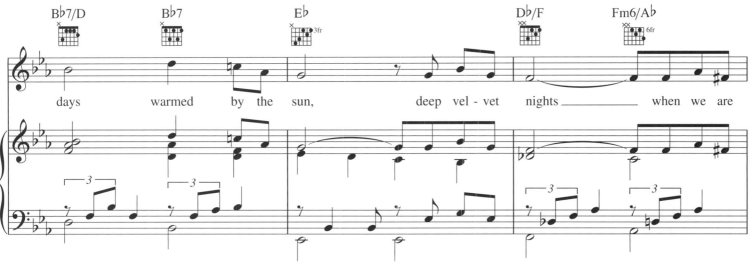

days warmed by the sun, deep vel - vet nights _____ when we are

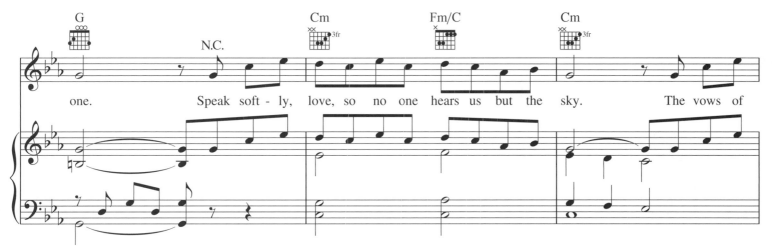

one. Speak soft - ly, love, so no one hears us but the sky. The vows of

love we make will live un - til we die. My life is yours _____ and all be -

cause you came in - to my world with love so soft - ly, love. Speak soft - ly, love.

TAKE MY BREATH AWAY
(Love Theme)
from the Paramount Picture TOP GUN

Words and Music by GIORGIO MORODER
and TOM WHITLOCK

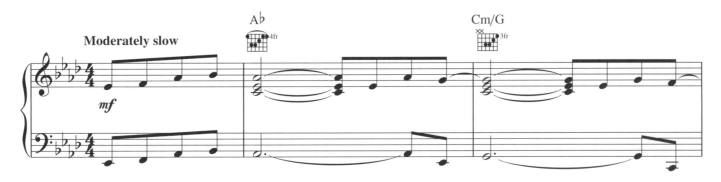

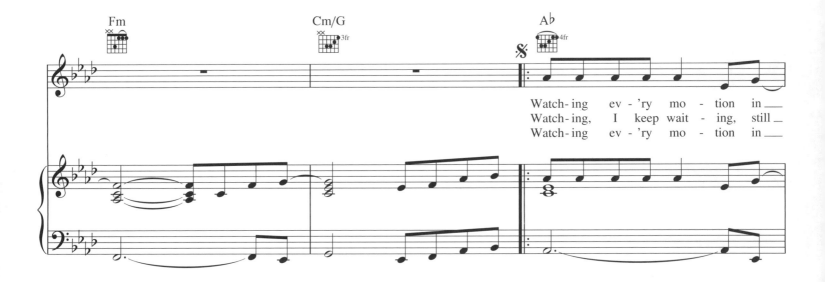

Watch-ing ev-'ry mo-tion in ___
Watch-ing, I keep wait-ing, still ___
Watch-ing ev-'ry mo-tion in ___

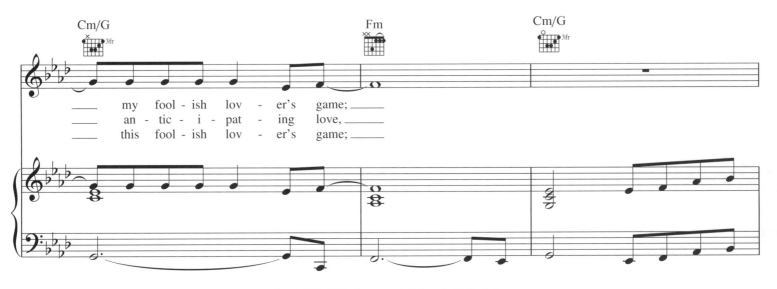

___ my fool-ish lov-er's game; ___
___ an-tic-i-pat-ing love, ___
___ this fool-ish lov-er's game; ___

on this end - less o - cean, fi - n'lly lov - ers know no shame._____
nev - er hes - i - tat - ing to_____ be - come the fa - ted ones._____
haunt - ed by the no - tion some - where there's a love in flames._____

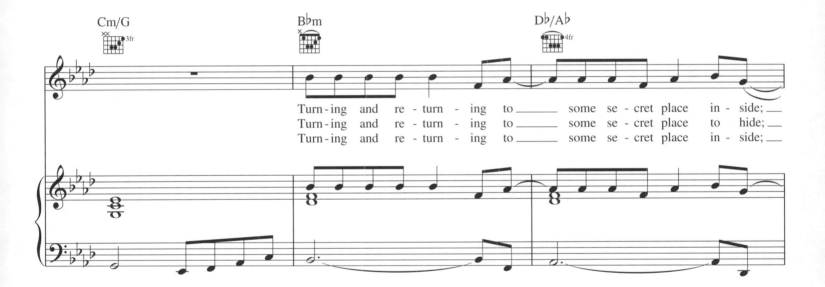

Turn - ing and re - turn - ing to_____ some se - cret place in - side;___
Turn - ing and re - turn - ing to_____ some se - cret place to hide;___
Turn - ing and re - turn - ing to_____ some se - cret place in - side;___

watch - ing in slow mo - tions_____
watch - ing in slow mo - tions_____
watch - ing in slow mo - tions_____

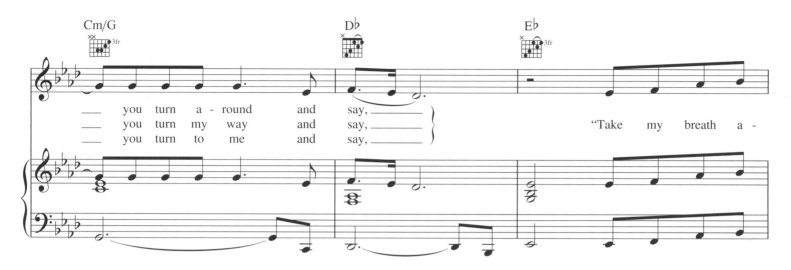

you turn a - round and say, _____
you turn my way and say, _____
you turn to me and say, _____

"Take my breath a -

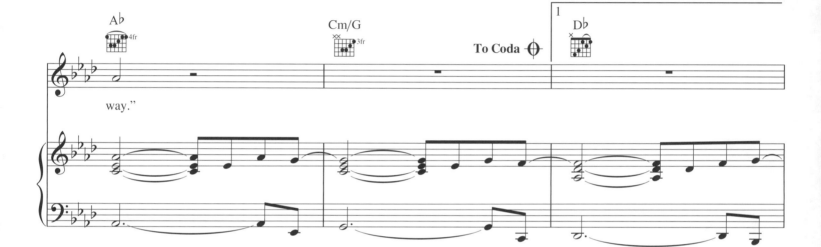

way."

To Coda

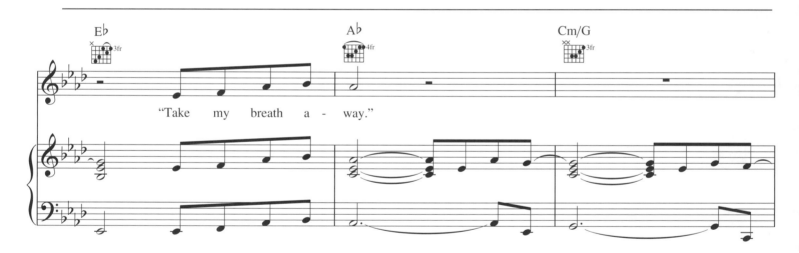

"Take my breath a - way."

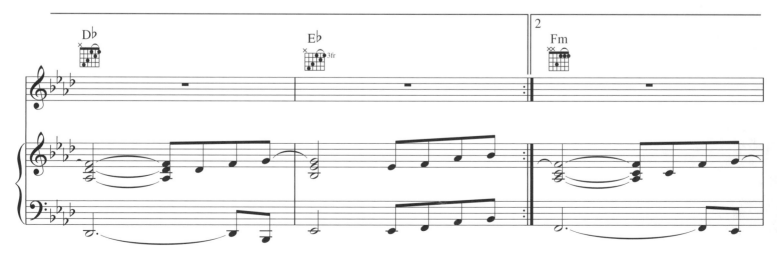

Through the hour-glass I saw ___ you. In time, ___

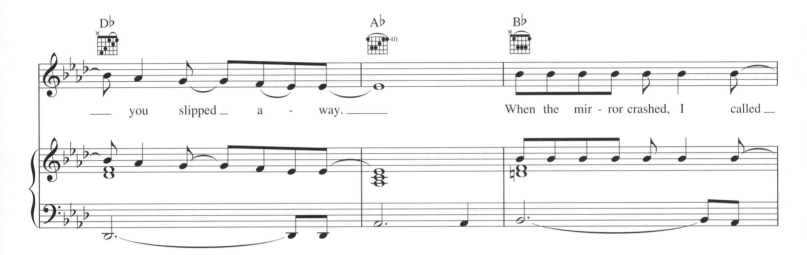

___ you slipped ___ a-way. ___ When the mir-ror crashed, I called ___

___ you and turned ___ to hear ___ you say, ___ "If on-ly for to-

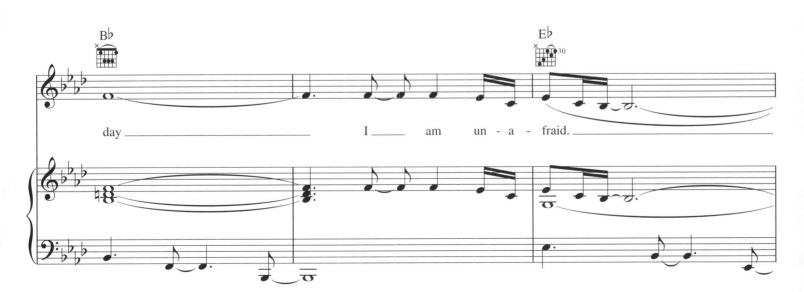

day ___ I ___ am un-a-fraid.

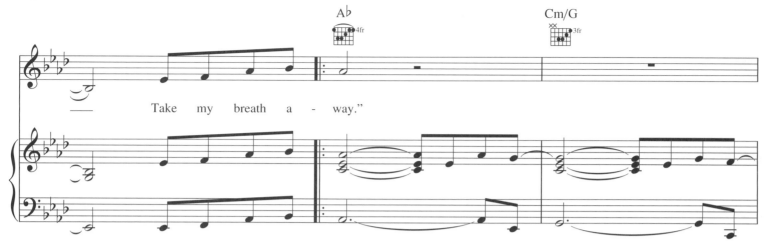

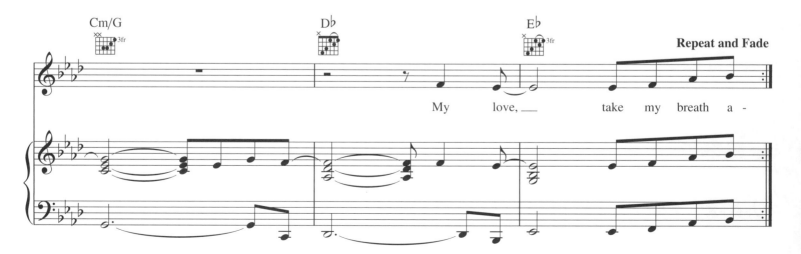

TEARS IN HEAVEN

featured in the Motion Picture RUSH

Words and Music by ERIC CLAPTON
and WILL JENNINGS

Would you know my name _____
Would you hold my hand _____
Would you know my name _____

if I saw you in heav - en?
if I saw you in heav - en?
if I saw you in heav - en?

Would it be the same _____
Would you help me stand _____
Would you be the same _____

190

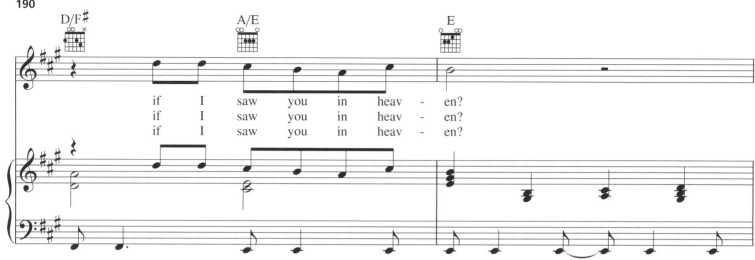

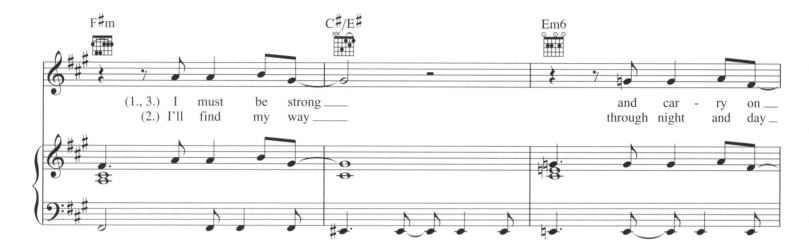

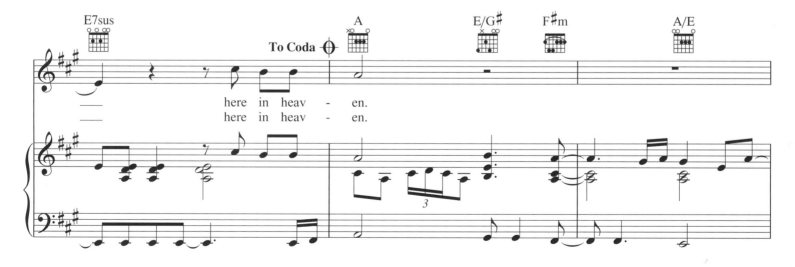

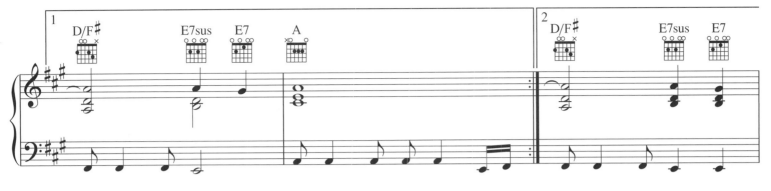

Time can bring you down, _____

_____ time can bend your knees. _____

Time can break the heart, _____ have you beg - gin' please, _____ beg - gin' please. _

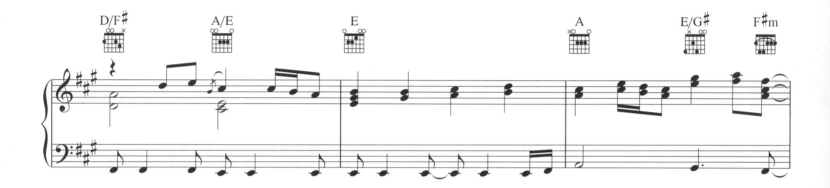

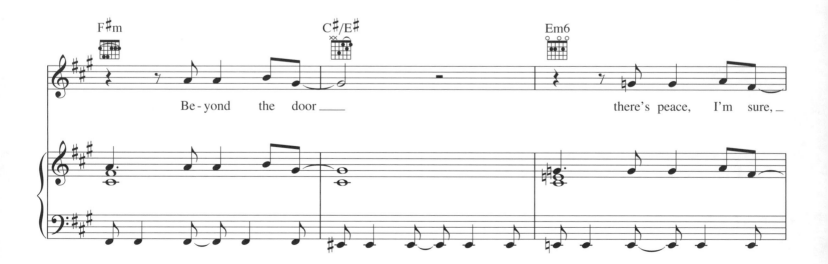

Be-yond the door ____ there's peace, I'm sure, __

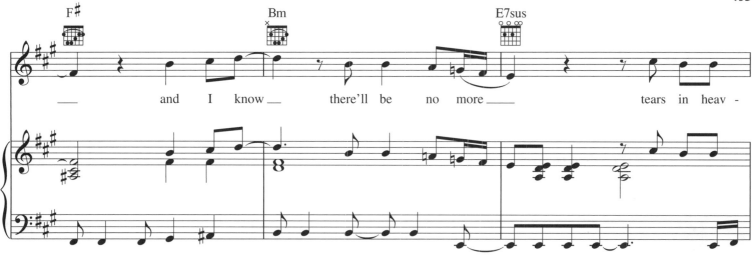

and I know ____ there'll be no more ____ tears in heav-

en.

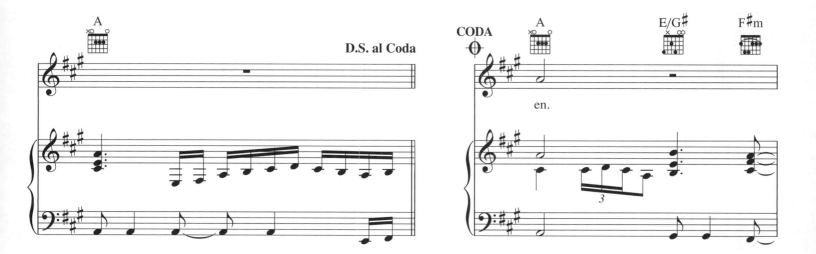

D.S. al Coda

CODA

en.

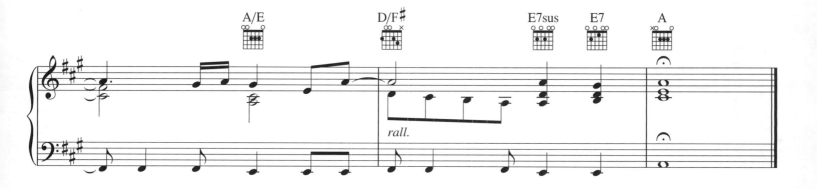

rall.

A TIME FOR US
(Love Theme)
from the Paramount Picture ROMEO AND JULIET

Words by LARRY KUSIK and EDDIE SNYDER
Music by NINO ROTA

Slowly and expressively

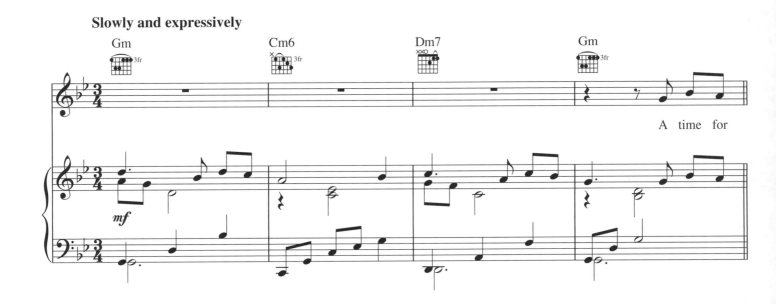

A time for

us some-day there'll be when chains are torn by cour-age

born of a love that's free. A time when dreams so long de-

nied _____ can flour - ish _____ as we un - veil the

love we now must hide. _____ A time _____ for us _____ at

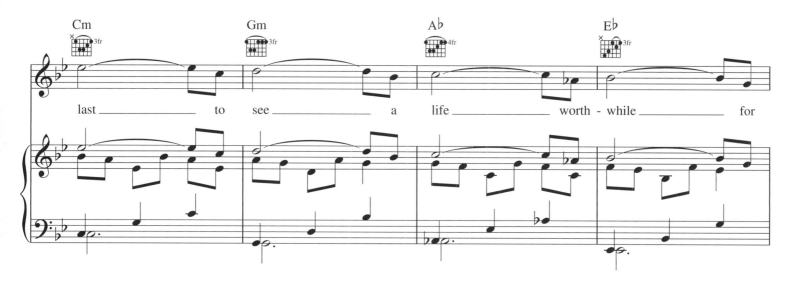

last _____ to see _____ a life _____ worth - while _____ for

you _____ and me. And with our love through tears and

TO SIR, WITH LOVE
from TO SIR, WITH LOVE

Words by DON BLACK
Music by MARC LONDON

Those school girl days of tell - ing
The time has come for clos - ing
Those awk - ward years have hur - ried

tales and bit - ing nails are gone, _____
books, and long last looks must end. _____
by. Why did they fly a - way? _____

but in my mind / And as I leave, / Why is it, sir,

I know they / I know that / chil - dren grow

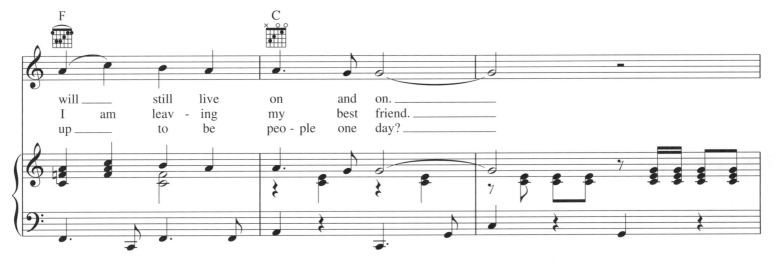

will ___ still live on and on. ___
I am leav - ing my best friend. ___
up ___ to be peo - ple one day? ___

But how do you thank some - one ___ who has
A friend who taught me right from wrong ___ and
What takes the place of climb - ing trees ___ and

tak - en you from cray - ons to per - fume.
weak from strong, that's a lot to learn.
dirt - y knees in the world out - side?

It is - n't
What can I
What is there

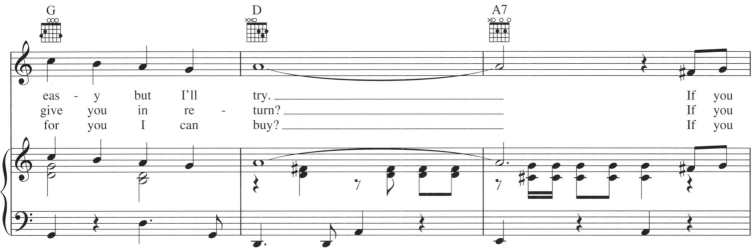

eas - y but I'll try. _____ If you
give you in re - turn? _____ If you
for you I can buy? _____ If you

want - ed the sky I'd write a - cross _ the sky in let - ters _ that would
want - ed the moon I would try to _ make a start, _____ but
want - ed the world I'd sur - round it with _ a wall; I'd scrawl _____ these

soar a thou - sand feet _ high _____ "To sir, _____ with
I would rath - er you let me give my heart _ to sir, _____ with
words with let - ters ten feet tall: _____ "To sir, _____ with

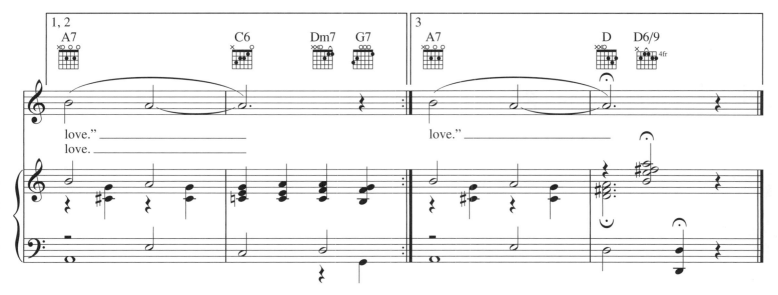

love." _____
love. _____

love." _____

(I've Had)
THE TIME OF MY LIFE
from DIRTY DANCING

Words and Music by FRANKE PREVITE,
JOHN DeNICOLA and DONALD MARKOWITZ

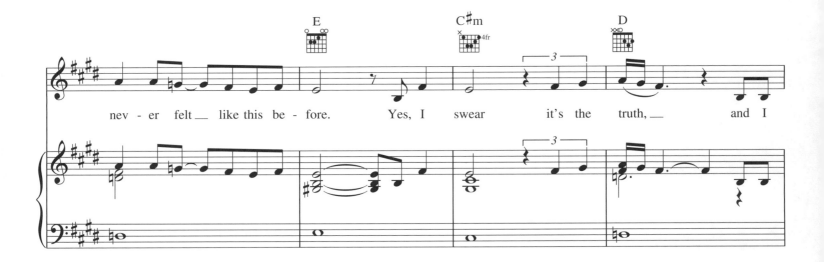

cy. *Male:* Just __ re - mem - ber, *Female:* you're the

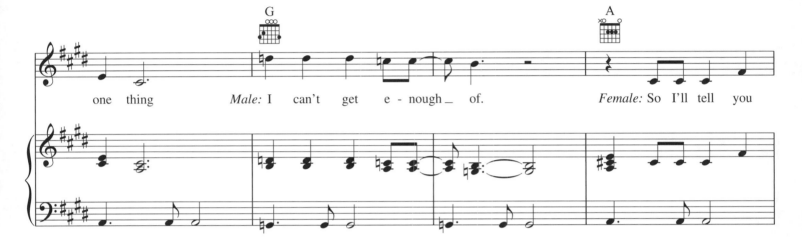

one thing *Male:* I can't get e - nough __ of. *Female:* So I'll tell you

some - thing: *Both:* this could be love. Be - cause I've __ had __

__ the time of my life. __ No, I nev - er felt __ this way be -

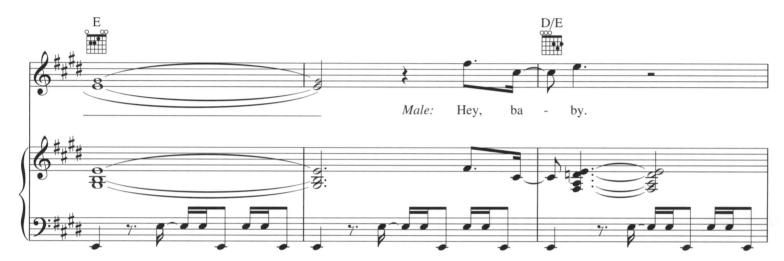

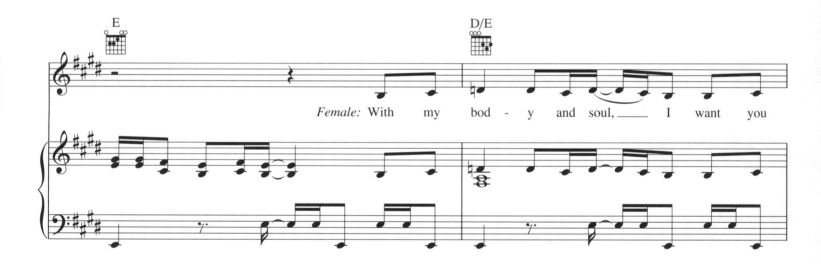

just let it go; ___ don't be a - fraid to lose con - trol. ___

Female: Yes, I know what's on ___ your mind when you say stay with me to-

night. ___ *Male:* Stay ___ with me. Just re - mem - ber, you're the

one thing ___ *Female:* I ___ can't get e - nough of. *Male:* So I'll tell you

some - thing: __ *Both:* this could be love. Be - cause I've __ had __

I've

__ the time of my life. ____ No, I nev - er felt __ this way be -

had the time of my life. ____ And I've searched through ev - 'ry o - pen

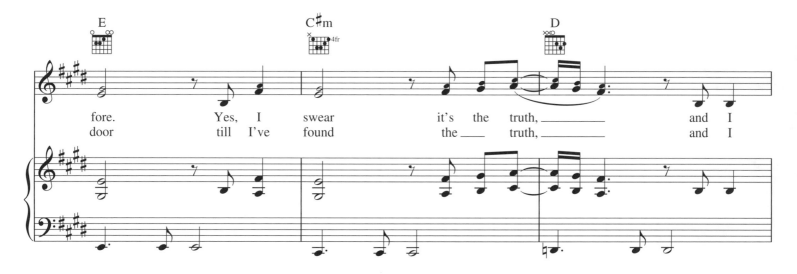

fore. Yes, I swear it's the truth, _____ and I

door till I've found the __ truth, _____ and I

owe it all to you. __ 'Cause __ owe it all to you. _____

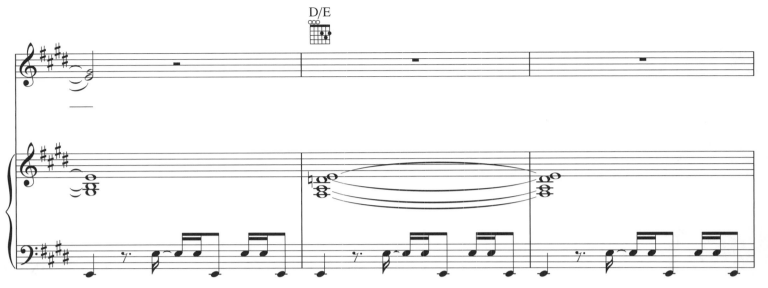

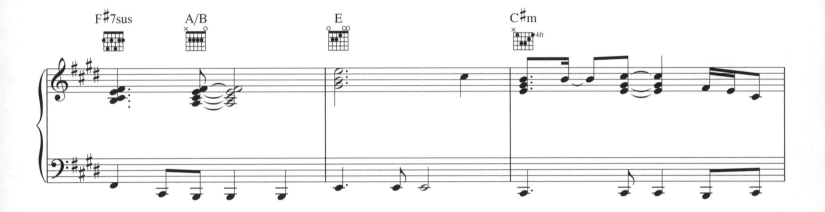

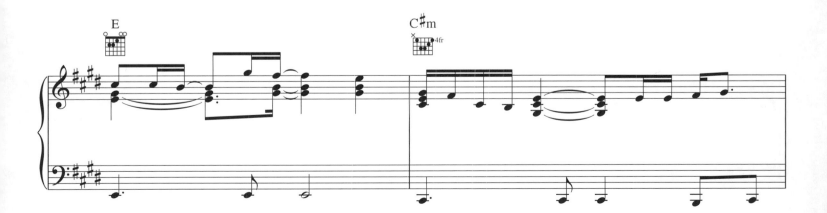

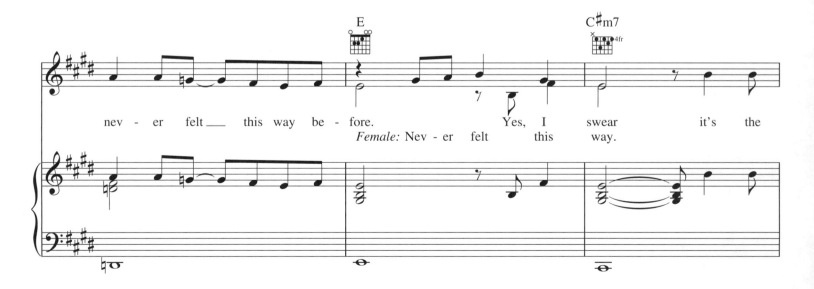

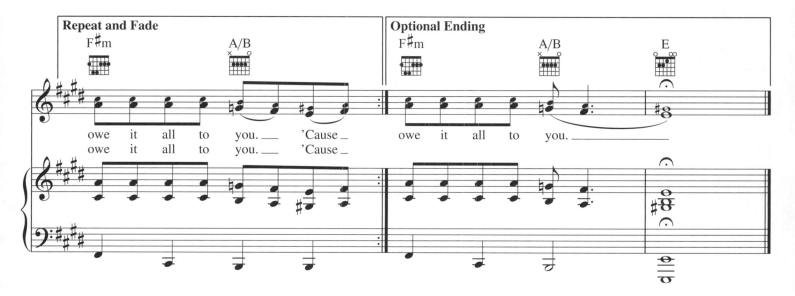

UNCHAINED MELODY

from the Motion Picture UNCHAINED
from the Motion Picture GHOST

Lyric by HY ZARET
Music by ALEX NORTH

Moderately slow

Lone - ly___ riv - ers flow   to the sea,   to the sea,

to the ___ o - pen arms _____ of the sea, _____ yeah. _____

Lone - ly___ riv - ers sigh,   "Wait for me, _____ wait for me.

THE WAY WE WERE
from the Motion Picture THE WAY WE WERE

Words by ALAN and MARILYN BERGMAN
Music by MARVIN HAMLISCH

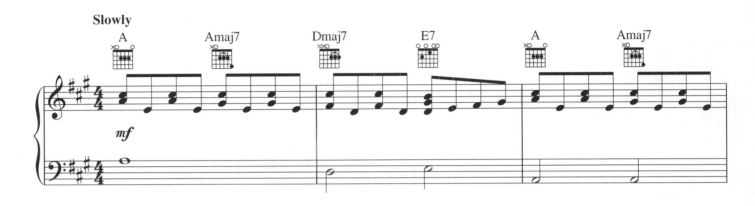

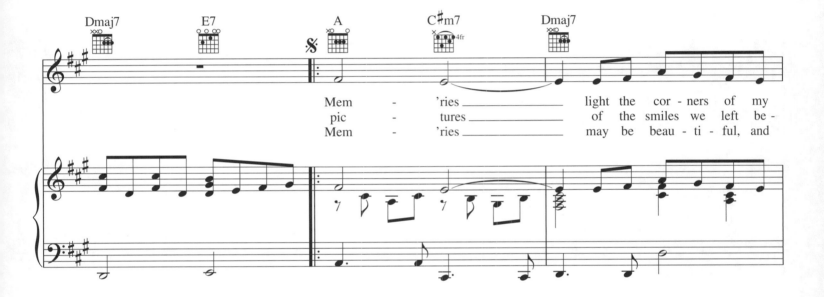

Mem - 'ries _____ light the cor - ners of my
pic - tures _____ of the smiles we left be -
Mem - 'ries _____ may be beau - ti - ful, and

mind.
hind,   Mist - y wa - ter - col - or   mem - 'ries _____
yet,   smiles we gave to one an - oth - er _____
         what's too pain - ful to re - mem - ber _____

of the way we were.
for the way we
Scat-tered

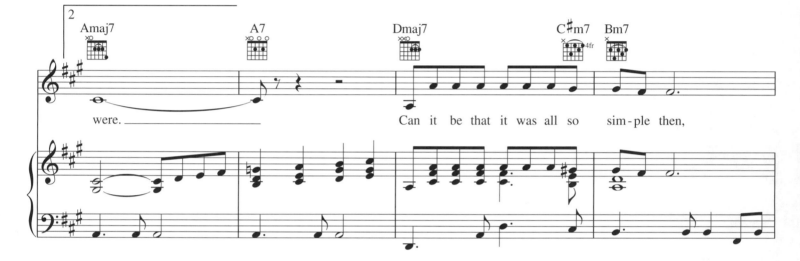

were. _____ Can it be that it was all so sim-ple then,

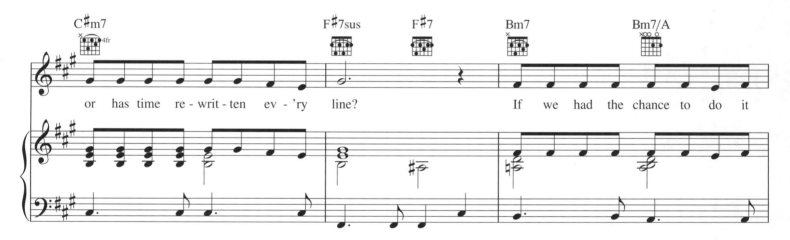

or has time re-writ-ten ev-'ry line? If we had the chance to do it

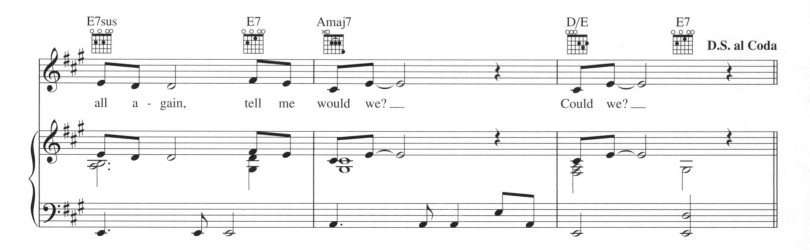

all a-gain, tell me would we? ___ Could we? ___

D.S. al Coda

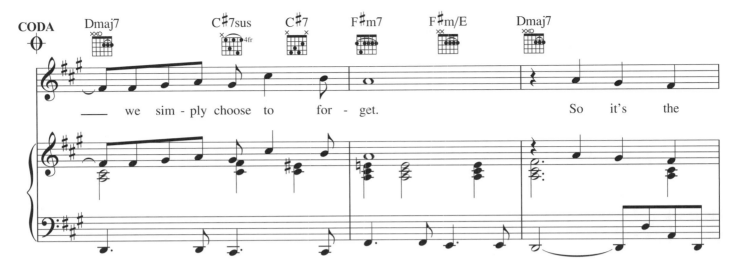

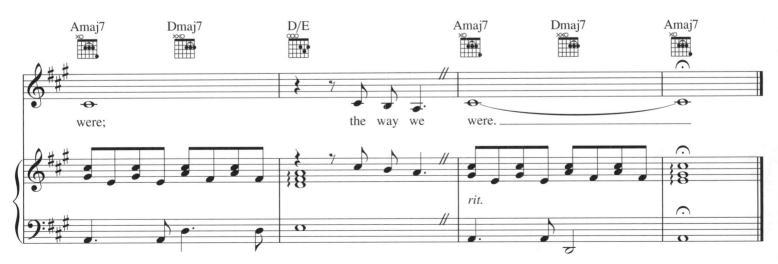

UP WHERE WE BELONG

from the Paramount Picture AN OFFICER AND A GENTLEMAN

Words by WILL JENNINGS
Music by BUFFY SAINTE-MARIE and JACK NITZSCHE

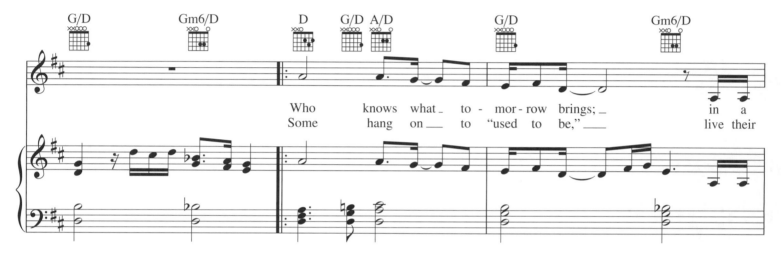

Who knows what to-mor-row brings; _ in a
Some hang on _ to "used to be," _ live their

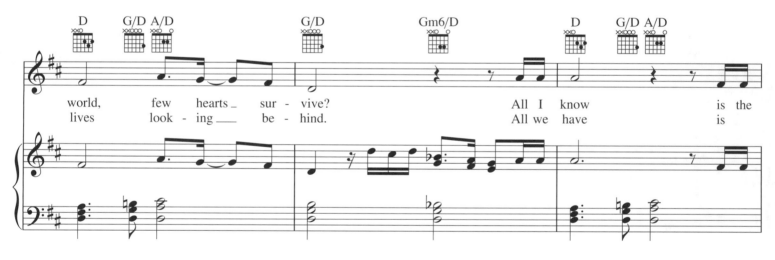

world, few hearts _ sur - vive? All I know is the
lives look - ing _ be - hind. All we have is

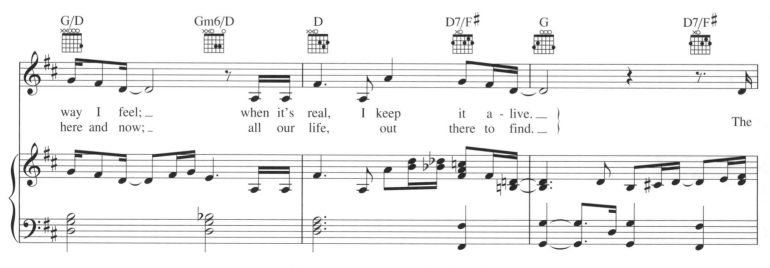

way I feel; _ when it's real, I keep it a - live. _ 〕
here and now; _ all our life, out there to find. _ 〕

The

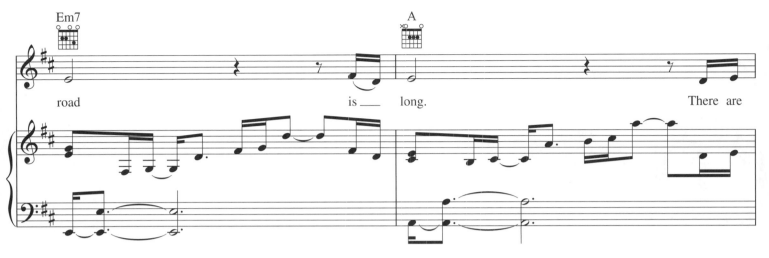

road   is ___ long.   There are

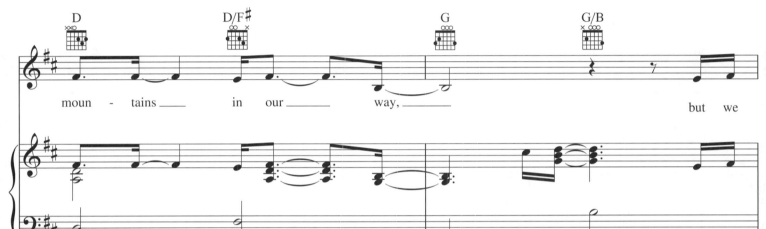

moun - tains ___ in our ___ way, ___   but we

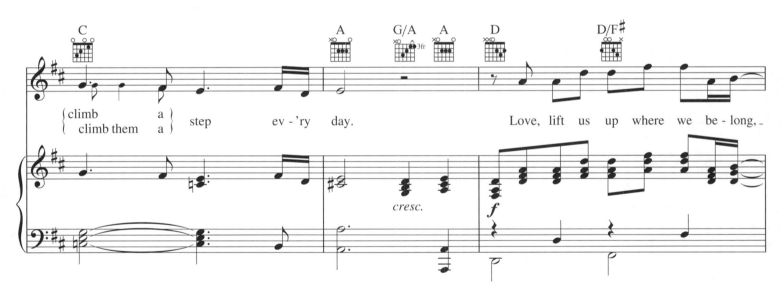

{climb   a} step   ev -'ry day.   Love, lift us up where we be - long, ___
{climb them a}

_   where the ea - gles cry ___   on a moun - tain high.

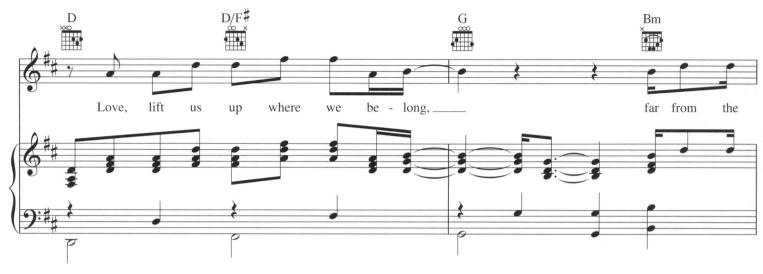

Love, lift us up where we be-long, _____ far from the

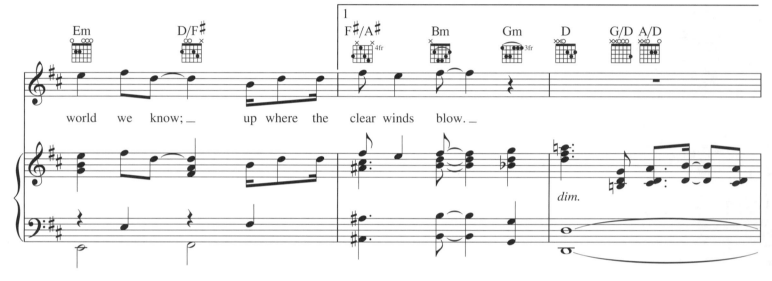

world we know; _ up where the clear winds blow. _

clear winds blow. ___ Time goes by, _

no time to cry, _____ life's you and I, ___ a - live, ___ to - day. _

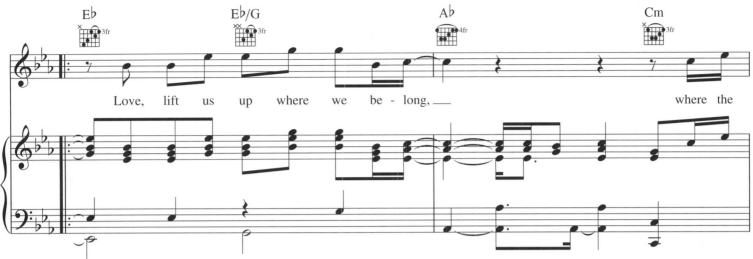

Love, lift us up where we be-long, ___ where the

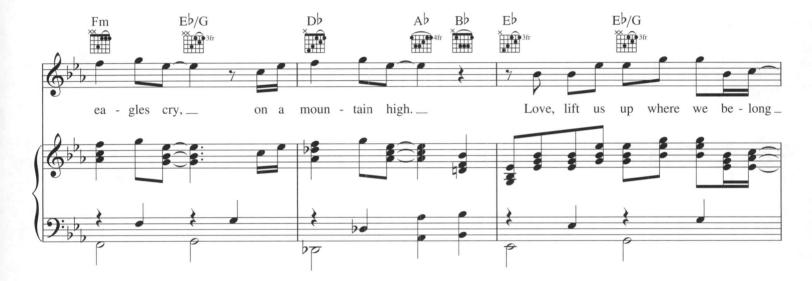

ea-gles cry, ___ on a moun-tain high. ___ Love, lift us up where we be-long ___

Repeat and Fade

___ far from the world we know; ___ where the clear winds blow. ___

Optional Ending

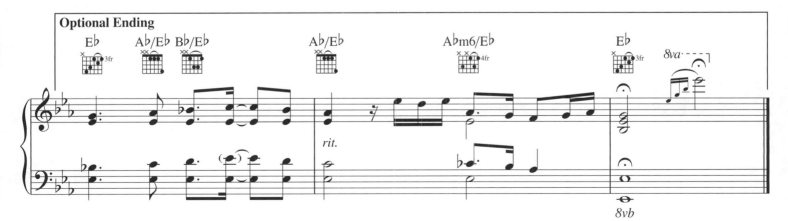

rit.

WHEN I FALL IN LOVE

featured in the TriStar Motion Picture SLEEPLESS IN SEATTLE
from ONE MINUTE TO ZERO

Words by EDWARD HEYMAN
Music by VICTOR YOUNG

heart. _____ Don't let me give my heart. _____ And ___ the

mo - ment I can feel _____ that _____ you feel __ that _____ way

too, _____ I feel that __ way __ too, is when I fall _____ in

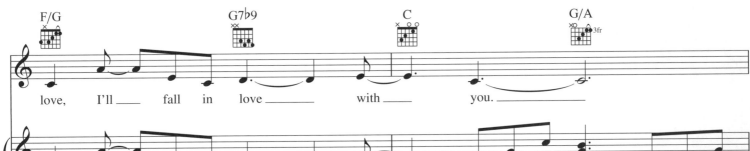

love, I'll ___ fall in love _____ with ____ you. _____

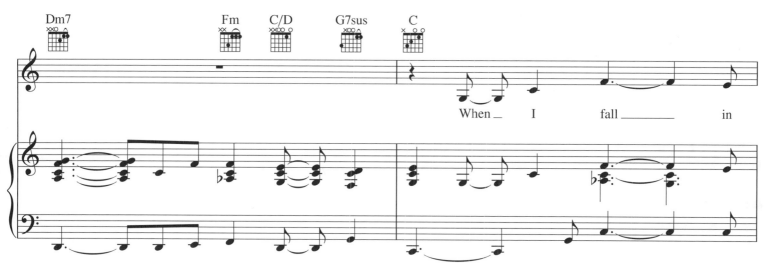

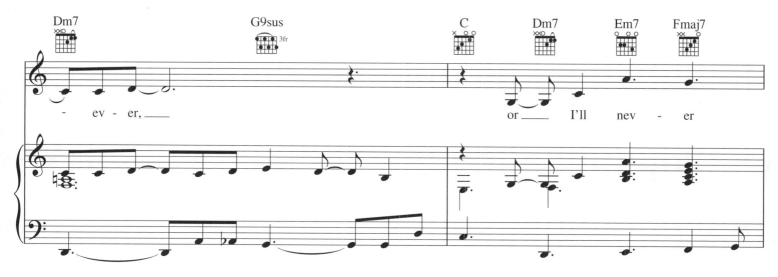

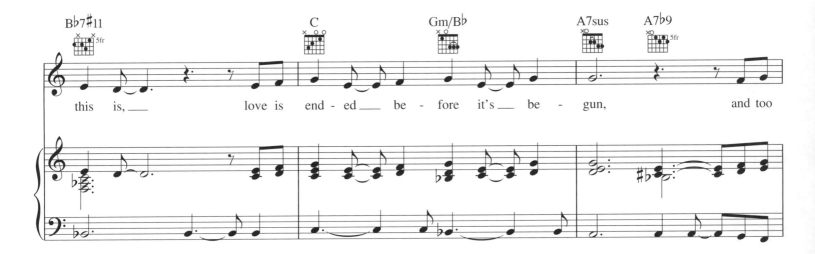

WHERE IS YOUR HEART
(The Song From Moulin Rouge)
from MOULIN ROUGE

Words by WILLIAM ENGVICK
Music by GEORGE AURIC

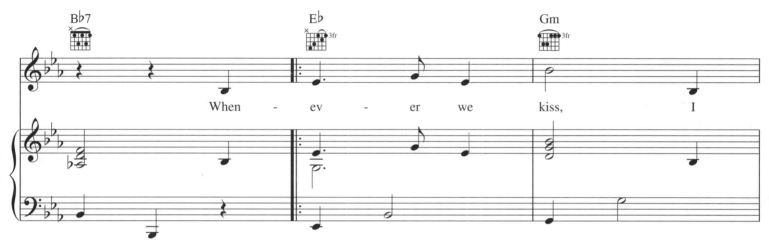

When - ev - er we kiss, I

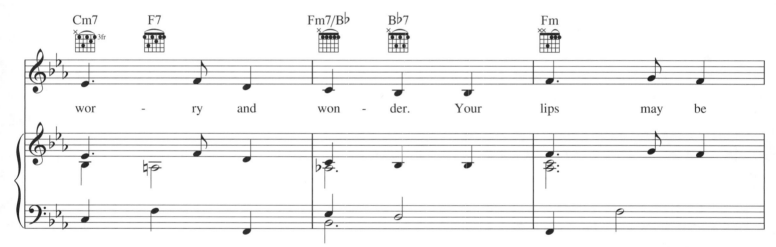

wor - ry and won - der. Your lips may be

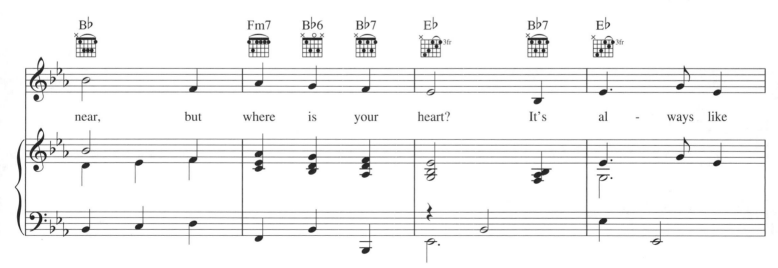

near, but where is your heart? It's al - ways like

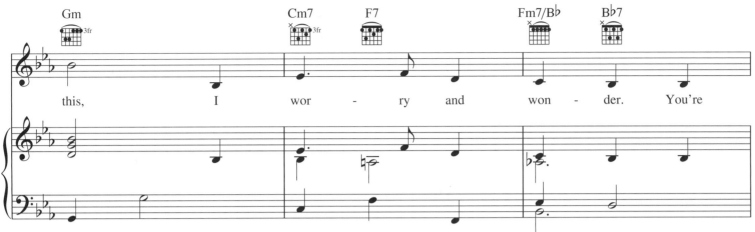

this, I wor - ry and won - der. You're

close to me here, but where is your

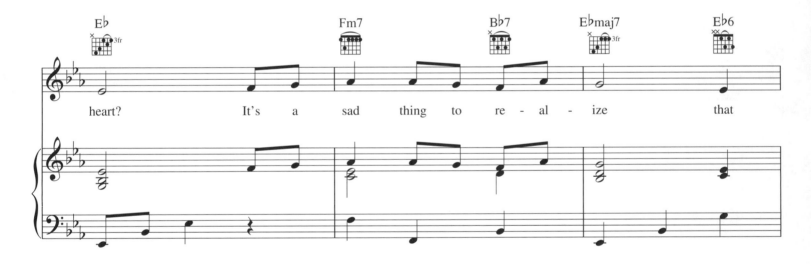

heart? It's a sad thing to re - al - ize that

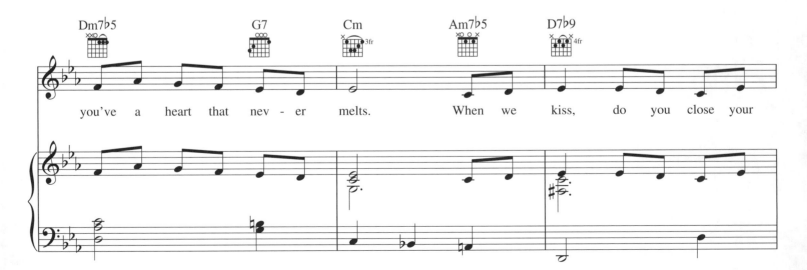

you've a heart that nev - er melts. When we kiss, do you close your

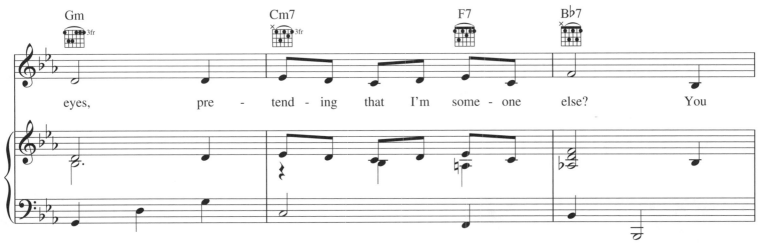

eyes, pre - tend - ing that I'm some-one else? You

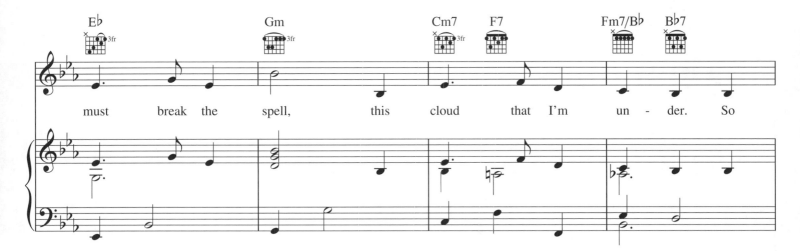

must break the spell, this cloud that I'm un - der. So

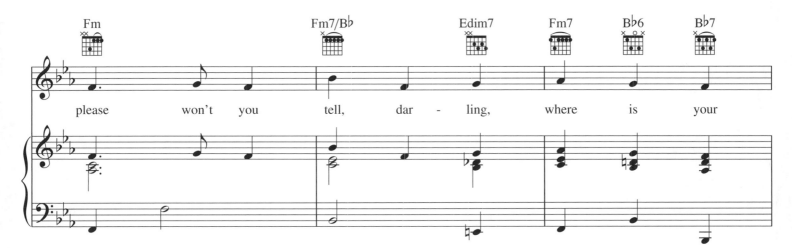

please won't you tell, dar - ling, where is your

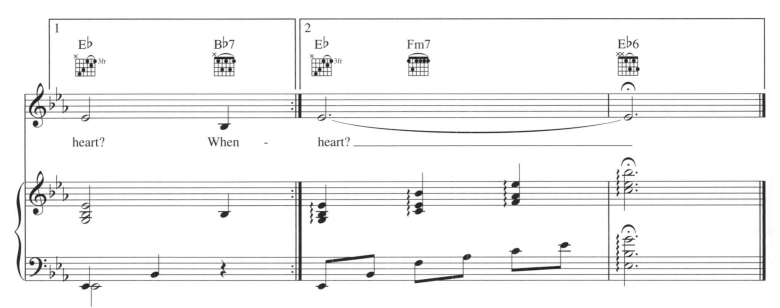

heart? When - heart? _____

WHERE DO I BEGIN
(Love Theme)
from the Paramount Picture LOVE STORY

Words by CARL SIGMAN
Music by FRANCIS LAI

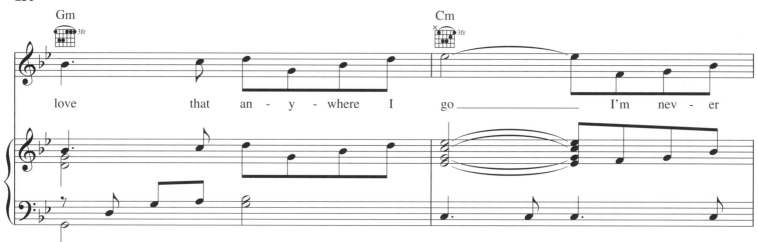

love that an - y - where I go _____ I'm nev - er

lone - ly. _____ With her a - long, _____ who could be

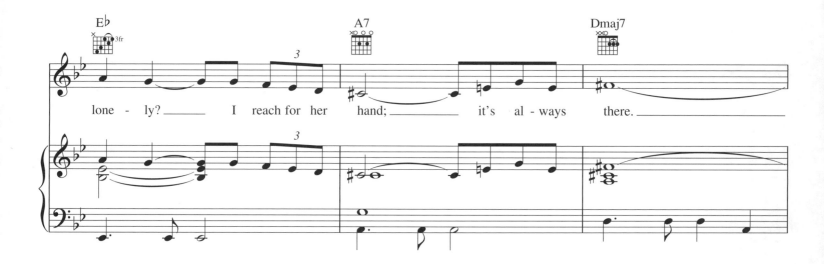

lone - ly? _____ I reach for her hand; _____ it's al - ways there. _____

_____ How long does it last? _____ Can love be meas - ured by the

ho - urs in a day? _____ I have no an - swers now, but this much I can say:

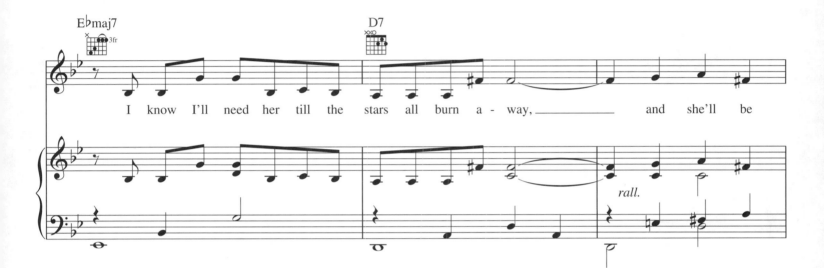

I know I'll need her till the stars all burn a - way, _____ and she'll be

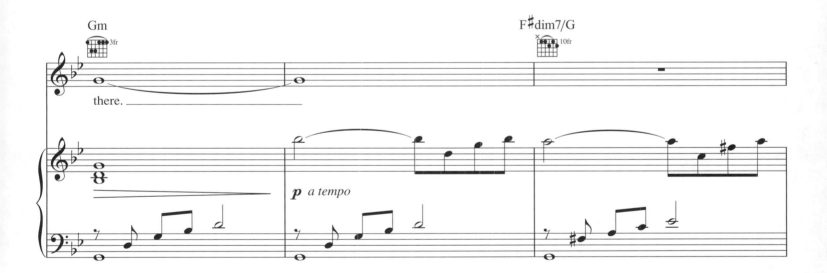

there. _____

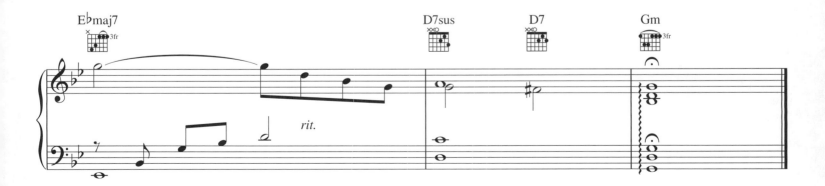

YOU MUST LOVE ME

from the Cinergi Motion Picture EVITA

Words by TIM RICE
Music by ANDREW LLOYD WEBBER

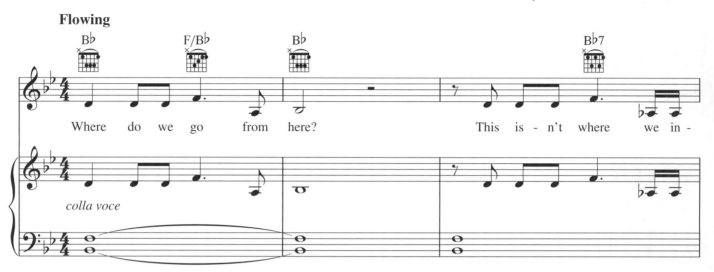

Flowing

Where do we go from here? This is-n't where we in-

colla voce

tend-ed to be. We had it all,____ you be-lieved_ in me,____ I be-

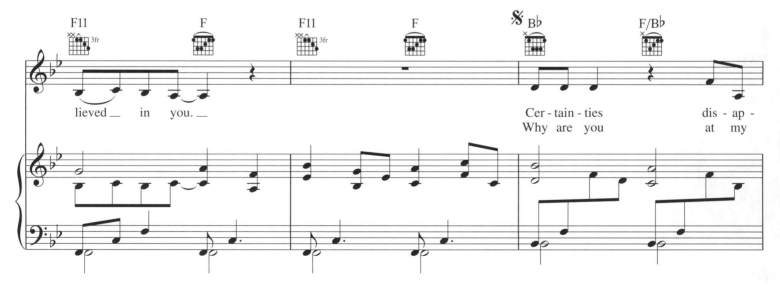

lieved_ in you.____

Cer-tain-ties   dis-ap-
Why are you   at my

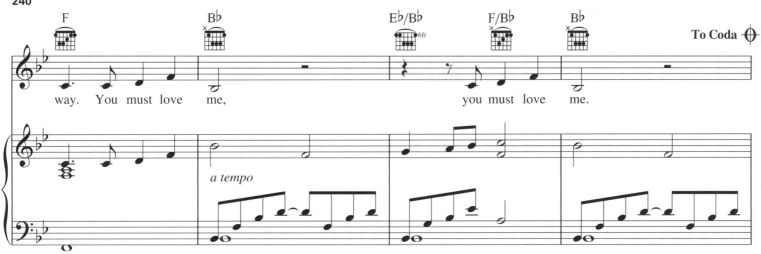

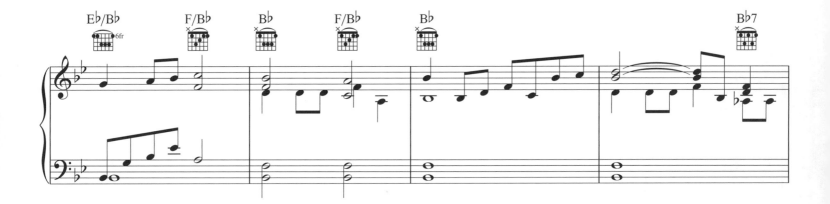

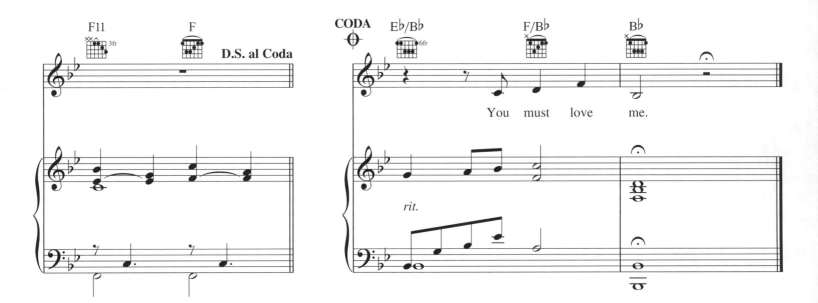